T0301576

THE LOGIC OF PROFESSIONALISM

Work and Management in Professional Service Organizations

Johan Alvehus

BRISTOL
UNIVERSITY
PRESS

First published in Great Britain in 2022 by

Bristol University Press
University of Bristol
1–9 Old Park Hill
Bristol
BS2 8BB
UK
t: +44 (0)117 954 5940
e: bup-info@bristol.ac.uk

Details of international sales and distribution partners are available at bristoluniversitypress.co.uk

British Library Cataloguing in Publication Data
A catalogue record for this book is available from the British Library

ISBN 978-1-5292-0606-7 hardcover
ISBN 978-1-5292-0607-4 paperback
ISBN 978-1-5292-0611-1 ePub
ISBN 978-1-5292-0609-8 ePdf

Cover design: Namkwan Cho
Front cover image: Shutterstock/mekebey
Bristol University Press uses environmentally responsible print partners.
Printed and bound in Great Britain by CMP, Poole

To Karin

[P]rofessionalism means doing it right even when it doesn't matter.

Daniel Polansky, *The Builders* (2015)

Contents

About the Author

Johan Alvehus is Associate Professor at the Department of Service Management and Service Studies, Lund University. His research spans leadership and management in private and public professional service organizations, and he has published in journals such as *Organization Studies*, *Human Resource Management Journal*, *Journal of Professions and Organization*, *Public Administration Review*, and *Leadership*. He also publishes on method and academic writing (for example *Formulating Research Problems*, Lund: Studentlitteratur, 2020).

Preface

When wrapping up this book project, I started asking myself: Why did I develop an interest in professional service work and professional service organizations? Of course, it has to do with trying to understand working conditions in today's world of organizations, and the role of professionalism in society – much of what this book is about. But on a personal level there's also another reason: I am basically curious. I have spent my working years at university (an immensely complex professional organization), in academic publishing, and as a consultant, and I have therefore encountered many of the issues covered in this book, skin deep. And, I believe that there exists a professional ethos that should be safeguarded. This does not mean that we should not problematize and question professionalism – quite the contrary. And that is what I do in this book.

Parts of this book are based on my 2012 Swedish book *4 myter om professionella organisationer* (*4 Myths about Professional Organizations*) but the changes in terms of both theoretical angle, and in terms of the literature covered, is different to the extent that this is a completely different work. In other words, the way I now understand these topics has changed quite a bit over the last ten or so years. And so it should.

In working on this book, I have had great help from my academic colleagues. A very warm thank you to Susanna Alexius, Mats Alvesson, Thomas Andersson, Olof Hallonsten, Gustaf Kastberg, and the anonymous reviewer for reading and commenting on this manuscript. Without you, many flaws would still be there. Thank you, Mehdi Boussebaa and Justin Waring, for engaging discussions on parts of the book. Thank you, Laura Empson, for constant dialogue.

Another very warm thank you goes to Paul Stevens at Bristol University Press, for believing in this project from the beginning, and for helping me push myself through it.

1

Work in Professional
Service Organizations

Lawyers. Physicians. Accountants. Finance analysts. Psychologists. Researchers. Management consultants. They are all examples of the gold-collar proletarians of our age – they are doing *professional work*. But what do these professionals actually do? And how is their everyday work organized?

Professional work is said to be the quintessential work of the knowledge society, involving high education demands, complex and challenging tasks, and a working life characterized by continuous learning and personal development. At the same time, we find claims that this professional ideal is crumbling. Increasingly professionals work in large bureaucracies and seem to have work conditions not very different from non-professionals. New forms of management are said to erode their independence, autonomy, and status. And frequently we see reports of overwork, fatigue, and burnout, also among elite workers. Despite all the presumed independence of professional workers, they are said to need leadership in order to be able to provide their services in a good way. And on top of this come high-profile scandals in finance, health care, auditing, and so on, undermining their status and legitimacy: How can professionals perform so badly when they're supposed to be so good, so *professional*?

In this book I will try to address questions such as these by exploring the practices that maintain and uphold what is often called the *logic of professionalism* (Freidson, 2001). But these questions are far from simple, and neither will the answers be. If you read the previous paragraph carefully, you will see that it is full of contradictory statements. We associate professional work with independence; yet professionals often work in large bureaucracies. We associate professional work with autonomy; yet professionals are increasingly subject to control. We associate professional work with individual competence and judgement; yet professionals supposedly need leadership. Such tensions will come back throughout this book.

This is also to say that professional service work and professional service organizations operate in an environment with often conflicting expectations from professionals themselves, from clients, from formally appointed non-professional managers, and from stakeholders such as governmental bodies and interest organizations. Professional work is often undertaken in a situation with entangled institutional logics, meaning that professional service organizations operate in an environment of complex, conflicting, and sometimes irreconcilable demands (Alvehus and Andersson, 2018). This situation challenges traditional values of professionalism, such as an emphasis on the individual worker's judgement and autonomy, and brings in issues of profit maximization, market orientation, and bureaucratic control. In summary, the logic of professionalism is often depicted as being under threat.

But the case is not quite that simple. Professionalism has been depicted as being under threat for more than half a century. Yet professions are still awarded status and high salaries, the increasing emphasis on the importance of higher education sets expectations of professional careers to pursue, and many occupations strive for professional status. In face of all threats, ideals of professionalism are still going strong.

Against this paradoxical backdrop, this book is set. The aim of this book is to explore, in detail, *the way in which the logic of professionalism is maintained in professional service organizations*, despite these threats. The theoretical contribution is twofold. One, I reconsider and reconceptualize key elements in the literature on professional service work and the management thereof. Two, I offer a terminology for understanding how the 'internal lawful autonomy' (Weber, 1915/1946) of professionalism is maintained in organizations. The outcome of this is a quite sceptical view of the way in which professionalism is enacted in contemporary organizations.

For this endeavour, I need a theoretical entry point. In the book I will draw extensively on the idea of an institutional logic. An institutional logic is, briefly, 'a systematic way of thinking that can embrace and order most of the issues with which they deal' (Freidson, 2001, pp 6–7). I will return to a more extensive theoretical discussion of the institutional logic of professionalism in Chapter 2. For now, suffice to say that an organization dominated by professional logic is characterized by a highly autonomous workforce, working with applying abstract expert knowledge to clients' problems, that is very client-oriented and where the individual professional has extensive freedom in developing client relations, and where authority is more oriented towards knowledge expertise than formal bureaucratic hierarchies. We find such organizations in law, accounting, medicine, teaching, management consultancy, architecture, and so on. There are of course variations, and normally an organization will not live up to all of these criteria. Moreover, some organizations and occupations show similar traits but are not recognized as professions; I will expand on this tricky question in Chapter 2.

I have, however, one overarching concern with the extensive literature on institutional logics in professional service organizations. This concern is the lack of attention to the everyday work of professionals. I will develop this in detail, but already at this point, it is necessary to raise the question. Work, and the nature of work, is a key element in the understanding of society and organizations. Organization and management theory however seem to have taken an interest in structures, strategies, identities, culture, leadership, and so on – but work is notably absent. Barley and Kunda's (2001) call for 'bringing work back in' to organization studies still stands. Most discussions on professional service organizations cover topics such as the nature of professionalism, how professionalism relates to managerial initiatives, leadership and governance, hybrid structures, teams, human resource management, knowledge management, identity, and so on. All of course valid and interesting topics, well worthy of study (see Empson et al, 2015b). Yet, the lack in this field of research of an in-depth discussion of work, and the nature of professional work, is striking.

A similar point can be made regarding different forms of management and control. These are often described in terms of their systemic character, and less often in terms of how they actually operate in organizations. But we must remember that management is also work – it is the work of managing other work (Weber, 1968, p 114). As such, we need to understand both professional service work and the management of professional service work at the 'coalface', that is, from a detailed understanding of everyday life work and management, 'where the rubber of theory hits the road of reality' (Barley, 2008, p 510).

Professional service work, and the work of managing professional service work, is thus my second entry point. It is also the main topic of this introductory chapter. Later in the book, in Chapters 3–6, I will continue to explore work and management through four different topics: work and ambiguity (Chapter 3), control (Chapter 4), leadership (Chapter 5), and hybridity (Chapter 6). In these chapters, by closely engaging with the literature I show that many of the ways in which we think around these topics need to be reconsidered. At the end of the book, in Chapter 7, I will get back to the topic of how professionalism is created and reproduced in professional service organizations, and I will finish the book by speculating on the future of professionalism in Chapter 8.

In this introductory chapter, I will set the stage for the rest of the book. First, I introduce the idea of professionalism in the context of what is commonly referred to as the knowledge society, and following from this

I expand on the concept of professional service work, opening up for a problematization of the four key topics that await.

Knowledge work and professionalism

It is often said that we live in a knowledge society or a knowledge economy, with a corresponding claim that this puts new demands on the workforce in terms of education and competence, and on organizations in terms of knowledge management and learning. Management guru Peter Drucker coined the term 'knowledge work' in 1959. So, the idea that there is a 'shift to knowledge as the foundation of work and performance' (Drucker, 1969, p 355) is more than half a century old. We should be well into this knowledge society by now and, undoubtedly, knowledge and information have come increasingly into focus in the search for competitiveness and success. Heralded by the work of scholars such as Manuel Castells (1996, 1997, 1998) and Shoshana Zuboff (1988, 2019), we are perhaps entering an age where knowledge, information, and big data are becoming the key factors of production. Although the substance of such claims of 'entering a new era' should always be problematized, we can at the minimum say that the discourse of the knowledge society has had a profound impact on how we view organizations, work, and employment.

In some ways the trends are paradoxical. On the one hand there are visions of a society with ever-increasing knowledge among the broad population; on the other hand, there are visions where power and knowledge become a currency held by the few – or end up belonging to machines. Knowledge-intensity often implies that the knowledge in question is 'advanced' but we should remember that 'advanced' is a relative term – it means that the client or consumer has little insight into the exact nature of knowledge and its applications. Whether such knowledge asymmetry (Sharma, 1997) should be understood as based on real differences or as based on image-work and mystifications has been debated (Alvesson, 2004). For the purpose at hand, suffice to say that today, many different types of work are understood as knowledge-intensive, meaning that the work is based on, in relative terms, advanced knowledge applied to products, research and development, or to clients' problems.

Many such types of work aspire to be *professional*, thereby signalling that performing the work and evaluating the outcome of the work is something only those well trained for the task can do. Moreover, professional work is often related to ideas of a broader contribution to society; professionals, it is then claimed, do not primarily strive for profit, but for the *summum bonum*, the common good: physicians strive to lessen human suffering, lawyers uphold justice. Such claims, direct or indirect, however, deserve to be received with some scepticism. As noted by Watson (2002, p 102):

> the notion of a special kind of knowledge-based occupation or 'learned profession,' which would retain much of the prestige and standard of living enjoyed by the 'gentleman' professionals of the pre-capitalist period, was the creation of nineteenth-century medical, legal, and church men who wished to keep themselves above and beyond the grubbiness of commerce, competition, and the profit motive.

Already at the outset, then, professionalism has been part of inter-occupational struggles for power, recognition, status and position in society, and other rewards. Today, the term 'professional' is not exclusive to 'classic' professions such as accounting, law, university research, and medicine. Where the line is drawn is less clear. What about high-school teachers, or kindergarten teachers? Or police, or social workers, or management consultants? Is there something that these all have in common? And what about a former chartered accountant now working with internal financial control at a municipality?

Many occupations strive to be recognized as professional, and many organizations emulate forms of working and organizing found in professional organizations. There are also ongoing efforts to professionalize tasks, for example various instances of management: general management, human resource management, project management, management consultancy, and so on. Traditionalists may warn against a dilution of the notion of professionalism. On the other hand, some occupations have allegedly become deprofessionalized and there are efforts to re-professionalize them. A case in point is teachers in Sweden (I will return to this example in Chapter 4). All in all, being 'professional' is a label that is attractive and it is still a key element in the struggle for recognition. It signals status, competence, and exclusivity, it holds a promise of escape from excessive bureaucratic control – and of course warrants high salaries. Some commentators see the struggle to become recognized as a 'profession' as a struggle to achieve high standards of knowledge and ethics, whereas others are more sceptical and see it as a vain struggle for recognition, status, and salary.

Looking at the sociology of professions, the 1970s saw a strong critique of the exclusiveness of professionalism. Larson (1977) argued that professions maintain their status by sustaining knowledge monopolies and making themselves unaccountable. From this perspective professionalism is understood as a way of withdrawing from external control and gaining status based on more or less arbitrary credentials. The counter-argument to this is the view that professionalism as a value and as a work ethic is increasingly jeopardized by external demands of control. 'Audit society' (Power, 1997) demands accountability from professions and organizations alike, and with the rise of New Public Management (Hood, 1991),[1] professions in the public sector have been subjected to detailed control systems as well as exposed to market mechanisms. From this view, professions and professionalism is under threat, and its unique contribution to society risks being undermined by bureaucrats and market mechanisms that ignore the complexity, ambiguity, and distinctiveness of professional work (Freidson, 2001; Styhre, 2013). What is less often remembered is the critique towards professions having grown too strong, and that public sector costs were seen as getting out of control and beyond political influence.

This polarization makes it a precarious task to define or even try to characterize professionalism. Definitions will award status to some occupations and exclude others. Saying that 'this is a profession' makes that statement itself part of the struggle for recognition and legitimacy of that occupational group. Thus, talking about professions and professionalism is, in and of itself, contested terrain – in Chapter 2 I will discuss in more detail how I deal with these issues. But, the contested nature of these terms is part of the reason I find this topic interesting. Ultimately, it concerns questions of power over work.

Professional service work

The key concern in this book is exploring practices that maintain and uphold the logic of professionalism. In the context of contemporary professionalism, it is thus a question of how and why we recognize some organizations as professional, and others not. My way of approaching this is using professional service work as an entry point. Therefore it makes sense to elaborate somewhat on what this is all about.

In fact, what is 'work'? When a lawyer tries to get all the minute details in a contract into place, we would certainly call it work. But how do we view that half hour after an exhausting meeting, spent loafing and mindlessly browsing the internet? When the lawyer asks her colleague for advice on a

---

[1] New Public Management (Hood, 1991) has been widely criticized. New Public Management, sometimes simply referred to as NPM, is a very broad term that tried to capture 'a general, though not universal, shift in public management styles' (Hood, 1995, p 94). This includes increased market-orientation and a belief that competition significantly improves efficiency, import of management and control forms from the private sector, and increased demands for accountability. The vagueness of the term has unfortunately led to critique being just as vague, and there are too few analyses that look into the effects of different, and sometimes contradictory, elements that are brought under the New Public Management umbrella.

clause, is this work? For both? Probably. But if it's advice on her own career development? Or what about socializing chit-chat over a cup of coffee that might perhaps forward her career by building relationships? And what if this chit-chat is done after office hours over a glass of wine?

The question of the nature of work has been debated for ages and the various approaches could be the topic of a book in themselves. (There already are such books, of course.) For example, we can understand work as those activities that are necessary for the material reproduction of society (in line with Marxian thought such as Kosík, 1976). This would invite critique of what we actually consider to be work today, such as 'bullshit jobs' (Graeber, 2018). Another way is to see work as related to what people themselves see as work, how people feel about what they do all day, and the meaning and significance it has in their lives (Terkel, 1974). Karlsson (2015, p 4) describes this as a dividing line between ontological and empirical conceptualizations, where 'the first one usually deals with the position of work in the life of human beings as species and for her development and survival' whereas the second is focused on the 'factual manifestations' of work in everyday life.

This book has a slant towards the latter definition, and I take the everyday experience of work and management as a starting point. However, this can of course never be understood completely outside relations of production, and the way in which work is managed and controlled. That said, the idea of this book is not to catalogue and classify different work activities of professionals. By giving work centre stage, I mean that the starting point for understanding the logic of professionalism and the management of professional service work is an understanding of the characteristics of professional service work. Moreover, being managed also involves work, for example taking part of different kinds of meetings or filling out reporting systems. The work perspective I take in this book is to understand everyday professional service work, but also the management of that work in its everyday practical sense. Such a view opens up for questions of agency, because when we approach such processes at the 'coalface' (Barley, 2008) it is impossible to shy away from how individuals tweak, reject and manipulate systems and situations to different ends. Human creativity continuously subverts the seemingly objective character of phenomena such as management and work.

As the book progresses, I will paint an increasingly complex image of the nature of professional service work and how it is managed, and from this I will discuss what the logic of professionalism is all about. But I need a starting point. Commonly, professional service work is attributed these characteristics:

- Professional service work is about the application of abstract knowledge.
- Professional service work demands continuous learning and development.

- Professional service work needs adaptation to clients, although in varying degrees.
- Professional service work is autonomous.
- Professional service work is difficult to evaluate for those outside the profession.

For this book, I will use these points as an initial broad characterization. Yet, this says very little about what professionals actually do. One answer to that is that professional service work largely concerns *problem solving*. What would professionals do other than solving their clients' problems? Lawyers solve juridical problems, physicians solve medical problems, teachers help pupils learn. There are of course other things that professionals do too. For example, management consultants provide legitimacy to managerial decision-making, and can also serve as scapegoats if something goes wrong. But of course, bicycle repair is also a form of problem solving: diagnose what is wrong with the bike, and remedy it.

What is central to professional problem solving is that it cannot be reduced to a distinct step-by-step process where generic and commonly available knowledge is applied to routine problems. It is here that we lose the bicycle repair – that can fairly easily be taught in a manual or in a YouTube video. But instruction is more difficult when it comes to professional work. Instruction manuals only provide the bare bones and are often fairly useless, other than as an introductory step. Simple and explicit models only provide rough guidelines on how to actually undertake professional work. An aspiring professional coming straight from university will find that there's still a lot to learn – the formal knowledge base is just the start. Professional problem solving is the *application* of specialist knowledge (Abbott, 1991; Empson et al, 2015a) and thereby involves judgement (Styhre, 2013). In addition it is also about building client relationships, investigating the characteristics of a specific client situation, and asking questions and obtaining information – it is about relationships and communication just as much as it is about knowledge and information. It is not always the case that the client has insight into the problem's causes and solutions – lack of such insight is often the reason to approach a professional in the first place.

The knowledge asymmetry between professional and client means that professional work is ideally based on high standards of quality and ethics. It harbours a notion of craftmanship where the work in itself is meaningful and where there 'is no ulterior motive in work other than the product being made and the processes of its creation' (Mills, 1951/2002, p 220; see also Sennett, 2008). Whereas this somewhat romantic view of work in general has become obsolete in many cases – Mills argued already in the middle of the 20th century that it 'is confined to minuscule groups of privileged professionals and intellectuals' (1951/2002, p 224) – the notion of craftsmanship is still a core element in professional service work and the management of it. However, in such discussions, we must remind ourselves of the criticism levelled against professionalism and the struggle for exclusivity mentioned earlier. Aspirations to high standards are also a way of raising oneself onto a pedestal and launching more or less legitimate demands for status and recognition.

Problematizing the management of professional service work

If professional service work has the characteristics already noted – abstract knowledge applied to clients' problems, in a state of continuous development, autonomous, and difficult to evaluate – this should cause some real problems for the management of professional service organizations. Key resources – applied knowledge and client relations – reside in the heads of workers. Outcomes are difficult to evaluate. Autonomy means that it is difficult to intervene in the work process. Professional work seems the perfect anti-management storm. Yet, it is easy to see that there must be some sort of management going on in large professional service organizations. Hospitals, universities, multinational firms with tens of thousands of employees – of course they are not completely unmanaged. And as anyone holding a professional job in such an organization knows, management is often all too present.

Professional service work can be, and is, managed. But through its characteristics, it presents a number of challenges. These have been dealt with in the literature, and in this book I will discuss them in four separate themes. These were hinted already in the introduction to this chapter, but in the following they are put in more theoretical terms.

Professional service work is often understood to be ambiguous and, as mentioned, therefore difficult to manage. In Chapter 3, I will investigate this assumption, and my conclusion is that the ambiguity is as much an outcome of management processes as it is a cause of it. Ambiguity also seems to fulfil important functions, for example in professional training.

The second theme is control, and quite obviously, professional service workers are subject to a multitude of control mechanisms. In Chapter 4 I dig into a few of these. However, when reviewing the literature, it also becomes clear that professionals are often very skilled at taking active roles in the management of organizations, thereby exerting control over control.

In Chapter 5, I explore leadership. This is something often seen as problematic: leading professionals, it is claimed, is like herding cats. I argue, however, that this might indeed not be the case, but that in order to understand leadership in professional contexts – and for that matter, leadership in general (Alvehus, 2021) – we need to look also at the political, 'dirty' side of leadership.

Today, due to the observation that many professional service organizations operate in complex institutional environments, it is often claimed that they are becoming hybrid organizations that in different ways try to reconcile conflicting institutional logics. The way in which this ends up varies. Some argue that it is a steady march towards deprofessionalization, others that it is about the emergence of new organizational forms. In Chapter 6 I explore three different views on hybridity, but instead of trying to integrate or debunk them, I argue that the notion of superficial hybridity can explain why all three views might paradoxically be right at the same time.

Thus, in each of these four chapters I aim to take a fresh look at aspects of professional service work and the management of professional service work that are already quite familiar. My aim is to shed new light on them, and I think that giving work the centre stage allows for a more nuanced understanding of the dynamics underlying the management of professional service work. Each of these four chapters in a sense lives a life of its own in that it addresses slightly different areas of research that have developed somewhat independently. They can therefore be read in any order, although I have of course aimed at achieving some sense of progression throughout the text as a sort of reward to the obedient reader.

In Chapter 7 I take my observations one step further. As is apparent throughout the text, there is great variety in the way in which professional service organizations work, and in the way professional service work is managed. Often professionalism is seen as being under threat. Yet, it seems to be surprisingly resilient over time. In Chapter 7 I discuss how the logic of professionalism is maintained, and more precisely what it is that is maintained. I do this by introducing the terms *functional ambiguity* and *opaque transparency*. As those terms only appear at the end of the book, I will postpone the definition and theoretical basis of them for now, and only return to them when they come to the fore.

This book also has a normative ambition. As indicated earlier, I do believe that there are certain values in professionalism that need to be defended. Professionalism is to some extent a moral category that encompasses important values in society: a commitment to knowledge, to altruism, to prioritizing clients' well-being over profit. Doing one's best, to the best of one's knowledge and ability. This does not mean that we should put professional work on a pedestal; rather it means that we need tools to problematize and question the privileges that come with professionalism. To maintain the values of professionalism, we need to continuously critically examine and question professionalism. Chapter 8 is the book's coda, where

I will allow myself two liberties. First, I will speculate on the future of professional work in the light of current trends. Second, I will draw some normative conclusions about how we can relate to professional service work and what important lessons there might be also for work in general. Are there aspects of the logic of professionalism worth preserving?

Thus, the stage is set for the rest of the book. In the following pages, I cover a broad range of literature, on professions, professional service organizations, and on institutional logics. The terrain I am trying to cover amounts to – literally – thousands of books and academic papers, and any treatment of the topic will need to be selective. Borrowing an analogy from a famous hobbit, this means that in an endeavour such as this, to some readers the selection of literature will come through 'like butter that has been scraped over too much bread' (Tolkien, 1954/1994, p 34). But instead of trying to cover an area in its entirety (as if that would be at all possible), it is my intention to address a few key theoretical issues in order to problematize them. In doing this, I have continuously chosen to engage more deeply with fewer texts in order to develop my argument in detail. This does not mean that my argument does not aim to cover a wider terrain – it just means that I have deliberately aimed for an economical presentation, and that I have chosen in-depth engagement before broad sweeping overviews. To the extent that the approach I have chosen also helps to keep this book's page count down, I see it as an advantage.

2

Professionalism from an Institutional Logics View

In the previous chapter, I gave some starting points for the topic of this book regarding professional service work and how such work is managed. In this chapter, I will introduce a few theoretical terms that will reappear throughout the book, and in this I will also point out some caveats with these terms that are perhaps not always apparent. I will to some extent deal with definitions, and definitions are by their nature difficult beasts. On the one hand, we need them in order to know what we are actually talking about. Many concepts in the social sciences have broad use and can thereby become vague: culture, leadership, power, identity, to name but a few. When concepts become too broad and vague, they lose their analytical usefulness, in line with what Geertz (1973) once argued regarding culture: if everything is culture, the term culture no longer helps us to point to something specific and potentially significant.

On the other hand, too precise definitions make us lose sight of what we are looking for. Social phenomena are multifaceted and sometimes ambiguous, and precise definitions risk excluding aspects or instances that might help us learn, or make us see things a bit differently. For example, strict definitions of the term 'profession' risk excluding most occupations, leaving very little left to study and also making the definition too far removed from everyday uses of the term. Therefore, the terminology suggested here is best seen as 'sensitizing concepts' that 'suggest directions along which to look' (Blumer, 1954, p 7). The direction is hopefully clear, yet in empirical instances things will inevitably get a bit blurry.

This chapter takes the form of a discussion between concepts around professions and professionalism, and the abstract theory of institutional logics. I start off by discussing the term 'profession', and recognize a need for a more detailed way of discussing the characteristics of professionalism. In order to develop this I first engage with the theory of institutional logics, drawing on Freidson's (2001) framework, to set the stage for a more distinct discussion of professionalism and its relation to markets and bureaucracy. After this, I turn to discussing the kind of organization – professional service organization – that is in focus in this book. I summarize these theoretical influences in what I have chosen to call a 'Janusian' view on institutional logics.

The problems of defining 'professions'

A technical problem when making definitions is that one inevitably comes up against borderline cases. Take teachers. They are (hopefully) well educated, their work in the classroom is fairly autonomous, their primary interest should be the learning process of each pupil – all characteristics often attributed to professional work. Yet their work is constantly scrutinized and questioned by school managers and parents, and politicians will always want to have their say regarding the curriculum and thereby the work of teachers. Is teaching, then, a profession? Or a semi-profession? Or a pseudo-profession? Or is it 'merely' an occupation, like bicycle repair?

The terms 'profession' and 'professional' are in themselves rather vague, and can in everyday talk refer to many different things. Watson (2002) observes that 'professional' can mean, among other things: being paid to do something as opposed to doing it for leisure, as in being a professional bicycle repair person; that someone is especially competent in what they do, as in being a very professional social worker; or it can be someone working in an occupation formally recognized as a profession by demanding accreditation, such as being a medical doctor. Watson further notes that the opposite, being unprofessional, is associated with unethical and selfish behaviour – which is of course not the opposite of any of these. The common denominator seems to be that if someone is labelled 'professional', it is because they are particularly good or competent in something, and that professionalism has something to do with high ethical standards.

The example of teachers, and the observations made by Watson, illustrate some of the problems with the terms profession and professionalism, and thereby also with definitions. There is a danger in limiting the definitions too much, as it easily becomes so narrow that only a few occupations (medicine and perhaps some others) get though the eye of the definitional needle. If it is defined too generously, on the other hand, everything and nothing is a profession. We end up in endless discussions of whether certain occupations are professions, non-professions, or pseudo-/semi-/quasi-professions. Depending on definitions, it will award status to some and denigrate others – after all, who wants to be a non-professional or quasi-professional, or even worse, unprofessional?

These difficulties present a conundrum. Should social scientists abandon the term professionalism altogether, given its contested character, as suggested by Watson (2002)? At the same time, one could argue that in order to problematize professions and professionalism, we need to take the bull by the horns and talk about those very things. Otherwise, we (social scientists) put ourselves at risk of being seen as talking about something else than professionalism, and thereby the critique will likely miss its target. In this book I take the latter stance, choosing to talk about professionalism, but of course then running the risk of reifying.

However, I do so with some precautions. I will return to the characterization of professionalism in more detail in the next section, but before that my position needs to be elaborated in some more detail in relation to historical, spatial and conceptual dimensions of the study of professions and professionalism.

A common approach in the sociology of professions is to look at the historical development of professions in order to more clearly understand how their characteristics change, how they interact with each other and society in general, and, often, how they seem to be losing their autonomous character. Such studies have greatly improved our understanding of the contingencies of modern-day professionalism. Professionalism as a term appeared in English in 1541 and modern professions have their roots in the medieval guild system, but it was in the 19th century that occupations more strategically started to work towards the exclusiveness and recognition in society awarded by professionalism (Krause, 1996; Watson, 2002). Of course, societal division of labour into formally recognized occupational groups is (literally) ancient: In both the Roman Republic and the Empire, many occupations were highly organized and they were a political force to be reckoned with (Liu, 2013); in Genghis Khan's Mongolian empire occupations such as lawyers, scholars, undertakers, doctors, and priests of all religions were recognized – and liberated from taxes (Weatherford, 2004). Arguably some kind of division of labour into communities of practice, or into caste, class, or similar systems, is part of any human society, albeit with differing degrees of recognition and different ways of maintaining legitimacy. There are also many parallels to be made between traditional craft work and professional work (some of which I discuss in Chapter 3). Another example is the notion of hybrid organizations, that is, organizations dealing with multiple institutional logics (the topic of Chapter 6) – it is easy to argue that such hybrid forms have always been around. Continuing with ancient Rome, policing and security in the city of Rome was an, albeit not very efficient, hybrid between state efforts, community militia, and individual responsibility (Kelly, 2013). Such observations aside, however, the phenomenon of professionalism as we know it today is tightly tied to the modern state and modern capitalism, as these have changed the conditions of existence of professions. Compared to traditional guilds, modern professions are more dependent on state support and market mechanisms to the extent that they 'hardly seem to exist as unified entities in their own right' (Krause, 1996, p 283). Thus, we have to be careful when extending the parallels to times past.

That said, this book is less concerned with professions than with professionalism. Whether a certain occupation or profession belongs to or has grown out of a 'profession proper', whatever that is, is less important than if the work of the professionals is undertaken in professional service organizations, or if they directly or indirectly claim to provide a professional service.

Another issue that directly relates to how we define and understand professionalism is the geographical dimension. Are professionalism and professions similar across the globe? In general, discussions on professionalism have had a heavy emphasis on the West, and all too often the medical profession in the United States is in focus. Of course, it is problematic to take development there as symptomatic of global development. The example of journalism illustrates how taking a global perspective challenges assumptions of a unified professionalism (Waisbord, 2013). Studies of global professional service firms in management consultancy have shown how difficult it is to actually establish homogeneity across the globe even within an organization, yet the globalization of such firms is intricately intertwined with processes of economic globalization, and effectively the firms become agents of this (Boussebaa et al, 2012; Boussebaa and Faulconbridge, 2019). Another example is how economists have become globalized, and have done this largely without changing. At the same time they have contributed to homogeneity in economic structures worldwide (Fourcade, 2006). Globalization and how it relates to professionalism is an interesting, complex, and important issue, as of yet underexplored. Clearly, however, there is a need to sustain an awareness of the geographical scope, as well as occupational specificity, when it comes to statements about professionalism.

Yet another dimension is what aspect of society we look at when discussing professions and professionalism. Professionalism is a phenomenon that is broader in scope than pertaining to work and management alone. Professionalism can of course be understood in terms of broader social categories, for example to the extent to which it influences and maintains division of labour in society, and the role it plays in shaping people's identities and life-trajectories (Mills, 1951/2002; Terkel, 1974; Bourdieu, 1977). This book touches on such issues (see, for example, the discussions on identity in Chapter 4), yet professionalism in this broader sense is not my primary concern. The theoretical resources provided by the sociology of professions are here drawn on in order to address the admittedly less overarching, yet just as interesting (at least I think so!), questions of work and management in the everyday life of so-called professionals.

Insights from limitations such as scope in historical, spatial, and theoretical terms encourages any analyst to be careful when making generalizing statements. In this book, I discuss professionalism in a contemporary Western context, with attention to issues of work and management in and of professional service organizations. These reservations thus limit the scope of my argument. Yet, they do not solve the definitional issue; the question of what I talk about when I talk about professionalism, remains.

From professions to professionalism

One way of understanding professions is to, instead of making an 'essentialist' definition of what a profession is, discuss how different occupational groups create and maintain borders around their work: To try to understand why lawyers have been able to gain professional status, why teachers struggle to do so, and why bicycle repairpersons have yet been unsuccessful in this. (At this point I feel obliged to clarify that I am certainly not trying to degrade bicycle repair. Quite the contrary; as a cycling enthusiast I have nothing but the highest regard for competent bike repairpersons. They are invaluable.)

Borders around work tasks – *jurisdictions* – maintain a societal division of labour, and are vigorously defended by occupational groups (Abbott, 1988). Formal professional recognition, such as demands for accreditation by a professional body (for example, becoming a chartered accountant), is one way of strengthening jurisdictions by preventing non-professionals from delivering the same service. But the profession constantly needs to defend itself against other groups that claim to be able to solve the same problems that professionals do. By distancing itself from tasks that have become more trivial professions retain their status, for example when physicians' hand less advanced tasks over to nurses or when accountants try to move away from the fairly standardized task of accounting and instead move towards the more complex and lucrative business of giving advice and consulting. This also means that identifying the profession with a suitably vague and legitimate knowledge base, preferably connected to universities, becomes key, as such vagueness allows for mobility in the jurisdiction: the profession can move towards new tasks when old ones need to be abandoned to avoid trivialization. What 'counts' as a profession is then less an issue of definitions based on what a certain group of people do at a certain point in time, but can be seen as the outcome of struggles for status and recognition between different occupational groups. This view, forwarded by Abbott (1988), is analytically useful for understanding how professions develop and how professional jurisdictions shift over time. In fact, Abbott's view makes the question of what is a profession or not an empirical question – his approach encourages us instead to look to how recognized professionalism is an outcome of jurisdictional struggles. Therefore, it does not provide a very distinct point for our attention – it does not quite help us to differentiate between bicycle repair, management consulting, and medicine. Some would argue that there might not be a need for such a differentiation, and I would to some extent agree with this from an analytical standpoint.

Taking these reservations on board, we must be careful in regards to what we talk and write about when using nouns such as 'profession' or 'professional (worker)' as they reify and simplify what is actually a complex underlying process of legitimation and jurisdictional work, historically and spatially contingent. The social scientist can become hijacked in social actors' struggle for status and recognition (in the case of professionalism, see Watson, 2002; in general, see Giddens, 1984). I am in this book less focused on the question of whether certain professional groups warrant the label 'profession' or not, and I am therefore not concerned with pinpointing exactly what the characteristics of a profession are or should be. As indicated before, I prefer the adjective *professional* – professional work, professional service organization – and by such terms, I refer to occupations and organizations that encompass at least some characteristics that can be associated with professionalism. Yet, it becomes rather cumbersome to talk about occupations-that-aspire-to-being-formally-recognized-as-professions-or-already-have-become; therefore, I will use the noun 'profession' as a convenient shorthand for this.

The question that follows is of course how such 'professional' characteristics can be identified. For the practical purpose of wanting to understand the management of professional service work, and based on the idea that there might be something different or particularly interesting about this type of work (which I also agree with), we at the minimum need to establish what to look for. And for this, I turn to the notion of institutional logics.

Institutional logics

The term 'institutional logics' has become very popular in discussing professional service work and professional service organizations, and I will make much use of the term in this book.[1] The variety of work has, however, also produced a situation where the term 'institutional logics' suffers from a breadth of use and, with that, vagueness. There is a great

---

[1] This section draws partly on work I have been doing with Olof Hallonsten, Lund University. See Alvehus and Hallonsten (forthcoming).

difference between using the term to describe how actors draw on previous experiences to make inferences on how to behave in particular situations (Jackall, 1988), understanding them as ideal types (Freidson, 2001), and using them as representing 'constellations of relatively stable material practices' on a societal level (Thornton et al, 2012, p 129). Uses range from individual sense-making devices to abstract ideal types, and sometimes occur as an attempt to bridge both. An interesting dilemma for the institutional logics literature is its sometimes 'stuck in the middle' character. On the one hand, theories of institutional logics have been accused of inability to attend to 'the micro-level dynamics of institutions' (Zilber, 2013, p 81). On the other hand, institutional logics theories have been accused of being too focused on the individual level of meaning-making, and that such 'actor-centric' approaches turn notions of meaning 'into "tools" in cultural toolkits that actors can utilize strategically' (Meyer et al, 2021, p 181).

Commonly, institutional logics is associated with Friedland and Alford's (1991) attempt to 'bring society back in' to institutional analysis in organization theory. The term was already in use (see, for example, Alford and Friedland, 1985) but the 1991 publication is generally understood to be the starting point of the institutional logics approach. Friedland and Alford (1991) viewed Western society as comprised of several 'central institutions', for example the bureaucratic state, the nuclear family, and the capitalist market (p 232), all available to individuals as resources for both making sense of society and for action. Moreover, they envisioned the different institutional logics as 'both potentially autonomous and contradictory' (p 259) and therefore they become sites of struggle for individuals, groups, and organizations. From this, several directions have evolved, with diverging empirical approaches (Reay and Jones, 2016) and theoretical angles, yet in many ways key themes have been retained as starting points for the development of subsequent theorizing on the topic.

A fundamental theoretical problem for institutional logics theorizing is what these logics actually are. Building on for example Thornton et al (2012), many studies take institutional logics to 'exist independently of researcher's analysis of them' (p 511). Friedland and Alford strongly emphasized that institutional logics have both symbolical and material aspects to them, and sometimes institutional logics theory is positioned close to other theoretical concepts, which 'also complicates the delimitation of logics from similar concepts such as frames, interpretive schemas, or cognitive maps' (Meyer et al, 2021, p 173). Sometimes, as in Friedland and Alford's early conceptualization, there seem to be a not finite, but at least somewhat limited, number of logics. Friedland and Alford mention five, Thornton (2004) names six, and Thornton et al (2012) up the game to seven institutional orders: family, community, religion, state, market, profession, and corporation. Many studies have identified other logics, such as 'science' and 'commerce' (Greenwood et al, 2011), 'social welfare' (Pache and Santos, 2013), 'democratic' and 'managerial' (Blomgren and Waks, 2015), 'public' and 'civil society' (Alexius and Furusten, 2019), 'editorial' (Thornton, 2004), 'service' and 'goods' (Skålén, 2018), 'criminal punishment', 'rehabilitation', 'community accountability', and 'efficiency' (McPherson and Sauder, 2013) – and so on. There seems to be no end to the number of logics that can be found. Certainly, if logics are 'constellations of relatively stable material practices' (Thornton et al, 2012, p 129) that also exist on multiple levels (Thornton and Ocasio, 2008), we can expect a plethora of logics to be identified. A cynic could note that having a concept that invites ever-new logics to be identified and presented in academic papers of course is a way of generating more research output. The more general problem that arises is similar to that of institutional theory in general: 'institutions have become everything' (Alvesson and Spicer, 2019, p 205), and if everything is an institution, nothing is. The plethora of logics is however only one problem. Another lies at the very heart of how institutional logics are conceptualized.

In empirically oriented analysis, institutional logics are often conceptualized as tools 'available to individuals and organizations as bases for action' as suggested by Friedland and Alford (1991, p 253). Studies focus on for example 'how social actors translate logics into action' (McPherson and Sauder, 2013, p 166) or how they are translated, balanced, or enacted (Currie and Spyridonidis, 2015; Smets et al, 2015; Bévort and Suddaby, 2016; Alvehus et al, 2019a). What often begs an answer, though, is exactly *what* it is that is translated or enacted. Often this borders on tautology: A logic is defined in terms of a recurrent practice, and the recurrence of the practice is explained by an actor's use, translation, or enactment of that logic. Thus, it reoccurs because it reoccurs. Of course, actual studies are often more sophisticated than this, but it leads to theoretical difficulties, where a large toolbox of intermediate theoretical terms is drawn in, in order to establish the micro–macro connection (see the section 'A Janusian approach to institutional logics'). This in turn creates new entanglements, and unsurprisingly this take on institutional logics theory has over time become a very complex set of concepts and interrelations between concepts. In this, arguably, the theory loses some of its potential in that theorizing suddenly becomes more preoccupied with disentangling relationships between concepts and less focused on trying to engage with what it is that is going on in the world. We end up with impressive theoretical constructs, but the question is of what use they actually are: do they really help us see and understand things in society, already complex as it is? Does it encourage 'sociological imagination' (Mills, 1959/2000) or does it mainly open up for ever-increasing, self-referential theoretical musings?

My use of institutional logics in this book significantly deviates from the hunt for ever new institutional logics to be identified, and from system-building efforts. It sacrifices detail and theoretical sophistication for conceptual clarity, and I will develop this in what follows, first by introducing Freidson's (2001) take on institutional logics, and then by elaborating it further at the end of the chapter.

Market, bureaucracy, and professionalism

In this book, I will use Freidson's (2001) ideal-typical model of the logic of professionalism as a starting point for my understanding of professionalism. Freidson builds on the Weberian notion of an ideal type, a stylized theoretical model that is only partially concerned with empirical representation. Ideal types aim for 'the highest possible degree of logical integration by virtue of their complete adequacy on the level of meaning' (Weber, 1968, p 20) and are therefore concerned with drawing out key characteristics of the phenomenon at hand, allowing us to see if and how they manifest in empirical instances. However, because of the precision on the level of meaning, 'it is probably seldom if ever that a real phenomenon can be found which corresponds exactly to one of these ideally constructed pure types' (p 20). Thus, ideal types are at best an approximation and are primarily a tool for helping us see social phenomena. Ideal types help us direct our gaze.

Freidson's model comprises three such ideal types or *logics*: market, bureaucracy, and professionalism.

Freidson's three-part ideal-type model is explicitly concerned with identifying and differentiating the characteristics of professionalism, and is exclusively concerned with the organization of work in society. Other similar typologies and taxonomies exist that encompass a broader view of society and therefore include other areas: from Weber's (1915/1946) six value spheres (economy, politics, aesthetics, erotics, intellect, and religion) to Thornton et al's (2012) seven institutional orders. Any number of such spheres, orders, or logics can (as I argued earlier) of course be identified, and if approached as ideal types, it is rather pointless to try to prove whether they exist or not. The important question is whether they are useful or not – do they reveal something relevant for the question at hand? This is exactly why I choose to stick with Freidson's three logics, as they specifically help us approach the notion of professionalism in relation to two other modes of organizing work: markets and bureaucracies.

The logic of the market is perhaps the one most familiar. In a market, the customer has the ultimate decision over price and performance. If customers feel the service or product is worth its price, they will buy it. Providers of the services or products thus compete for the money of the customers, and to be successful they have to provide better price/performance offers, related to their costs. Success in the market is decided by the survival of the fittest providers – competition is the key mechanism. From a worker perspective, labour will have a market value and their skills will be sold to the highest bidder. In the case of standardized labour this will likely lead to a race to the bottom, as in the current-era gig economy (Standing, 2011), although such trends also appear in knowledge-intensive work (Barley and Kunda, 2004).

The logic of bureaucracy is characterized by formalized frameworks and legal-rational authority (Weber, 1968). In a bureaucracy, an administrative structure designs work tasks and evaluates performance and quality. This means that managers will have decisive influence over the organization of work, and through the managers the governing principal has indirect influence over the work undertaken. In contrast to the market, where customers are king and things are governed by an invisible hand, in a bureaucratic logic, managers are the prolonged hands of the governing body. From a one-eyed market perspective this way of organizing comes through as strange and inefficient – why not give people (customers) what they want, instead of what the governing body wants? Yet in many instances in society, we want this form of influence: police and social work would be examples. It is common to associate the logic of bureaucracy with the state and the public sector, but most companies are also bureaucracies: shareholders are principals, and managers execute their will by controlling work processes and outcomes. Thus, the dividing line between market and bureaucracy is not whether it refers to the private or public sector, but where ultimate control of work resides: '"Market" refers to those circumstances in which consumers control the work people do, and "bureaucracy" to those in which managers are in control' (Freidson, 2001, p 12).

The logic of professionalism refers to when workers are in control of the work process. Professional work is based on advanced knowledge, and the design and evaluation of work demands insight into this knowledge (in line with the characterization I gave in Chapter 1). Therefore, customers – in this context, clients – have great difficulties evaluating whether a work was well done and if the outcome was good. Professional workers' discretion and judgement are fundamental elements in the professional logic and this means that managers have little insight into work processes and that management is minimized. This even concerns control from professional peers, for even if they may have equal insight and competence in the professional work, the work also comprises adapting generic expertise to client's problems (cf Abbott, 1991) and, thus, the insight into the circumstances of each client's case is fundamental for evaluating work. This makes it impossible to entirely standardize professional work, even among peers. Instead, knowledge, client relationships, and judgement are key characteristics (Styhre, 2013). In summary, professionalism relies on monopoly (in contrast to market logic) and autonomy (in contrast to bureaucratic logic).

Formal professional bodies play a key role in maintaining the legitimacy of professionals' autonomy and task monopoly. By regulating entry and exit to professions they ensure that clients' ignorance is not exploited. They are key actors in granting formal credentials and in sustaining contacts with, for example, universities for legitimacy and status. Moreover, professional organizations often have codes of ethics and conduct that their members are supposed to adhere to, and on a symbolic level they provide elite identities. From society's point of view professional bodies provide the legitimacy needed for us to trust the professionals to be, well, professional, and keep the quacks and charlatans out.

It is of utmost importance to keep the ideal-typical character of professionalism, market, and bureaucracy in mind. Ideal types are useful analytical tools, but all three ideal types – market, bureaucracy, and professionalism – are 'pipe-dreams, of course. None of those worlds exist, and where some of their elements have existed, predicted virtues are always accompanied by unanticipated vices … Nonetheless, faith in those imagined worlds … lies behind policy choices' (Freidson, 2001, p 2). The ideal type of professionalism, applied to an occupational group, provides a source of legitimacy, warranted or not. The same goes for markets and bureaucracy. Taken as an *ideal*, rather than as an *ideal type*, professionalism becomes a powerful ideology in the contest between occupations for more privileges, more status, and more money, granting them a special place in knowledge society. That said, the main idea of this book is not to glorify professions or professional work, nor to downplay their relevance, but to problematize them and, thereby, hopefully, contribute to insightful policy choices.

Professional service organizations

Following the previous discussion, professional service organizations are organizations where professional work is undertaken. But this brings a key tension into the picture: If professional work is subjected to formal organizing – bureaucracy – does it not then follow that professional service organizations are subject to the logic of bureaucracy? And even more so, if it is a commercial professional service organization, does it not become subject to the logic of the market?

Yes, and yes. As stated before, empirical instances – such as a professional service organization – will always comprise several ideal types. Or more correctly put, we will be able to understand the patterns of action in them only through the lens of several ideal types. Therefore, there is today much talk about hybrid organizations, in order to try to capture the complexity and the tensions that arise from the coexistence of several conflicting logics. I will return to these questions in Chapter 6, and will therefore for the time being ignore them in order to introduce the notion of a professional service organization.

Professional service work, as characterized in the previous chapter, can take place almost anywhere. We can easily imagine solo professionals working independently – this is in fact an image of professional work that still prevails. On the other hand, many professionals work in large, capital-intensive bureaucracies such as university hospitals, others in larger but less capital-intensive firms such as global accounting or law firms. Thus, there are many organizational contexts where professional work takes place (von Nordenflycht, 2010).

Put simply, professional organizations are 'organizations in which members of one or more professional groups play the central role in the achievement of the primary organizational objectives' (Scott, 1965, p 65). This means that organizations where professional staff comprise only a small research and development unit would not be included; only those where they comprise the operating core of the organization would.

The term 'operating core' comes from Henry Mintzberg's (1979) famous typology, popularized in his book *Structure in Fives* (1983). To someone not familiar with Mintzberg's work, here's a crash course: Mintzberg divides the organization into five key parts. At the foundation of an organization, we find the operating core, the parts of an organization that produce the products or services that the organization delivers to its clients or customers. At the top, we find the 'strategic apex', where key decisions on, for example, resource allocation and strategy are made. Between these we find the 'middle line managers', essentially connecting strategies to everyday work through more operational decision-making, and by feeding information upwards. Next comes the 'support staff'. These parts of the organization provide services that are necessary for the organization to operate, but that do not per se affect the work flow. These include personnel departments, legal counsel, PR, and services such as catering and cleaning. Today, these are often outsourced, but are still part of the organization – the model focuses on flows of activities and information, not legal boundaries. Finally, the 'technostructure' is the function that designs and improves the processes in the operating core. In a classic industrial organization this would mean to develop and improve the production process, the machinery, and the internal logistics of the organization. Thus, the broad notion of 'bureaucracy' is present in all least four of the key parts of the organization: in management (strategic apex and middle managers), support staff, and technostructure. When discussing different organizational configurations, of main interest here are the 'professional bureaucracy' and the 'operating adhocracy' – and in those configurations the operating core plays a key role in determining how work is accomplished.

The definition of a professional service organization that I follow in this book, is, then: *service organizations where the operating core is dominated by professional logic*, including knowledge intensity, client-orientation, and autonomy in the design and evaluation of work. This also implies, as Mintzberg (1979) suggested, that professional organizations ideal-typically need very few middle managers and a minimal, if any, technostructure, as there is no need to exert managerial control over autonomous work. There is some need for administrative support, though, as professional workers are normally not very keen on doing work that is not directly related to what they perceive as their profession.

A slightly narrower concept than professional service organization is that of the professional service firm. This term, more established than professional service organization, is a useful point of comparison for outlining the professional service organization. In *The Oxford Handbook of Professional Service Firms*, the editors in the introductory chapter paint a broad characterization of what a professional service firm is. They start with what they see as the primary activity in the firm: 'Application of specialist knowledge to creation of customized solutions to clients' problems' (Empson et al, 2015a, p 6). A key phrase here is 'customized', and they further argue that it is about 'bespoke' services demanding 'intensive interaction' with clients (p 7). It is debatable whether for example a hospital or a school uses customized solutions; most of the time, likely not. A physician of course adapts treatment to the specific characteristics of a client, and teachers vary their pedagogic solutions to each pupil, but calling this customized would perhaps be drawing things a bit too far, and Empson et al (2015a) do not aim to cover these instances with their definition. But on the other hand, their definition aims to include, for example, large accounting firms and management consultancy. Yet, these both involve huge volumes of standardized work that is sometimes the 'bread and butter' of the business. And at least in the case of management consultants, there might be talk about client adaptation, but beneath this is sometimes hardly more than changed client logos on a PowerPoint presentation. Thus, just as regarding claims to knowledge intensity, claims to client orientation should be taken with a handful of salt (Alvesson and Spicer, 2016). Here I relax the 'customized' criterion a bit, and prefer to say that the degree of customization will likely vary between different types of professional service organizations (von Nordenflycht, 2010).

From their initial criterion follow three more, that are still of relevance for my discussion of professional service organizations. They concern knowledge, governance, and identity.

When it comes to knowledge, '[core] assets are specialist technical knowledge of professionals and their in-depth knowledge of clients' (Empson et al, 2015a, p 7). The first of these emphasizes the embodied and personalized knowledge of professional work. Even if the knowledge base of a profession is fairly generic, different professionals will have different hands-on experience. (If they did not, the need for a 'second opinion' would not occur very often.) Client-specific knowledge will depend on the degree of customization. Of significance is the personalized nature of knowledge. In so-called knowledge management, the idea is often to make individuals' knowledge into organizational assets, to turn human capital to structure capital. Professional service work generally disallows this.

When it comes to governance, professional service firms are characterized by '[extensive] individual autonomy and contingent managerial authority, where core producers own or control core assets' (Empson et al, 2015a, p 7). The demand for autonomy follows from the specialized knowledge. That professional work involves a high degree of judgement makes it difficult, if at all possible, to evaluate in standardized ways and with generic performance metrics. It also means that micro-management and strict managerial control becomes counter-productive. However, this appears only in an ideal-type world. Even in the most professional of professional organizations we will find performance metrics and control systems, for example, time, quality control, or standardization of tasks (see Chapter 4). Thus, and again returning to the ideal-type approach, we will likely not find this criterion in practice in a very extensive sense; yet, taken as an expectation or demand from workers, and in relation to even more controlled types of work, it is still relevant as a point of orientation. That core producers own and control core assets is particularly significant in professional service organizations operating with a low degree of financial capital, where the key assets disappear out the door at five o'clock (or, more realistically, quite a bit later). Some organizations that I include in the professional service organization umbrella are, however, capital-intensive; hospitals are a prime example. The knowledge of the professional worker is still the core asset, but in some instances it is not the only asset, and it is reasonably easy to replace it as client-specific knowledge is lower. Interestingly, then, the profession that is perhaps the most exemplary and common example of professionalism, medical doctors, often work in organizations quite far removed from what professional service firm definitions bring to the forefront.

The final criterion concerns identity (Alvesson et al, 2015). 'Core producers recognize each other as professionals and are recognized as such by clients and competitors' (Empson et al, 2015a, p 8). Professional identities are attractive as with them comes status and prestige. In some cases, this identity is well established in society – doctors and lawyers come to mind – and in others there is more of an ongoing struggle for recognition. Moreover, there might be tensions between professional and organizational identification, and sometimes identification with clients takes priority (Anderson-Gough et al, 2000). Traditionally, the emphasis on identity in professional service organizations is towards the profession per se, rather than towards the organization (Wallace, 1995). Identifying with the organization can be understood as both a way of lost legitimacy for professionalism (Evetts, 2011) and as a way of trying to increase the organization's legitimacy (Kirkpatrick and Noordegraaf, 2015). Within the context of professional service organizations, identity is not only a question of status, but also appears as a form of control. This goes hand-in-hand with classic ideas of management and control, stipulating that when it is difficult or expensive to both design work processes and measure outputs, control efforts will likely target 'soft' aspects such as culture and identity (Ouchi, 1979), paving the way for an extensive emphasis on leadership. I will return to this topic in Chapters 4 and 5.

For the remainder of the book, I will use the professional service organization as a somewhat broader category than professional service firm. While formally relying on the definition suggested – *organizations where the operating core is dominated by professional logic* – I find that Empson et al's (2015a) definition highlights key characteristics for this kind of organization, and a 'relaxed' version of their professional service firm characterization is helpful when developing the implications of the definition.

Again, I want to remind the reader that this is intended as a sensitizing concept. In the book, I deal with large bureaucratic public organizations such as hospitals as well as private enterprises such as small law firms. Differences in scope and scale will of course matter in terms of how each individual organization functions (Løwendahl, 2005; von Nordenflycht, 2010; Alvehus and Kärreman, 2019), and so will different institutional arrangements (Bourgeault et al, 2011), internal power balance (Scott, 1965), and of course the idiosyncrasies of individual organizations. Yet, as a starting point, we need to know in which direction to look, and for the purposes of the book, organizations where the operating core is dominated by professional logic gives such a direction.

A Janusian approach to institutional logics

It might seem as a long step between an ideal-type use of institutional logics, as in Freidson (2001), and what goes on, on an everyday basis, in a professional service organization. And, indeed, it is. We cannot deduct or in any detail predict individual behaviour from institutional logics; nor can we easily aggregate patterns of behaviour to logics. Ideal types, in the sense employed here, are theoretical devices that help us see how things 'hang together' in empirical instances. At the same time, the institutional logics refer broadly to patterns of behaviour – there has to be some reference point for them in order to be meaningful. And as patterns of behaviour are maintained by the action of individuals they are, at least in the long run, subject to change.

The problem lurking underneath this is the classic social science problem of structure and agency, dubbed the 'Gordian knot of the social sciences' by historians Jarrick and Söderberg (1991). Within the various traditions of institutional theory, there have been several attempts to untie this knot: Giddens' (1984) structuration theory, in organization studies fruitfully elaborated by, for example, Barley (1986) and Barley and Tolbert (1997); institutional entrepreneurship (DiMaggio, 1988); institutional work (Lawrence and Suddaby, 2006); some strands of institutional logics theory (Thornton et al, 2012; Ocasio et al, 2017); and inhabited institutions theory (Hallett and Ventresca, 2006; Hallett, 2010) – to name but a few. Commonly such approaches try to find ways of establishing connections between agency (action) and structure (patterns), and elaborate their interrelatedness in detail. The drawback is, however, the one I highlighted earlier: It tends to lead to theoretical systems that become overly complex. In the approach I take here I do not try to 'compete' with such efforts. Nor do I take Alexander's approach to the knot. Instead of trying to disentangle or cut the knot I am, for the purposes of this book, content with looking at it from different angles. This also means that I in no way draw on the idea of institutional logics as a theory of society in general; I understand it as a middle range theory, there to 'guide empirical enquiry' (Merton, 1968, p 39) and I put it to use for a specific purpose: understanding professional service work and management thereof.

Institutional logics, as I use the term here, should be understood as an ideal-typical way of systematically identifying recurring patterns of action. At the level of practice these will manifest as routines, habits, conventions, formal organizational structures, systems for control and resource allocation, and so on – much of what the next four chapters of this book are about. The point with understanding these as institutional logics is not that institutional logics per se exist, but that they provide a way of seeing what Weber (1915/1946) referred to as *Eigengesetzlichkeit*, 'internal and lawful autonomy' (p 328).[2] The idea with this 'internal and lawful autonomy' is that each institutional logic has its own rule set that applies to social action

---

[2] The term *Eigengesetzlichkeit* is not easily translated (Hallonsten, 2021) but for the purposes at hand, 'internal and lawful autonomy' as suggested by Gerth and Mills in their translation of Weber (1915/1946) suffices.

and to values within that logic – this is why it's useful to view it as a logic. Freidson's (2001) description of the three institutional logics illustrates this clearly with respect to control over the work process. Identifying the internal and lawful autonomy involves asking why a particular pattern persists over time. Sometimes this may be due to deliberate action (such as when managers formalize routines in organizations) but often it is a question of latent pattern maintenance (Merton, 1968), which means that the way in which the internal and lawful autonomy of an institutional logic works and the processes of its reproduction are unknown and unintended as far as the actors are concerned.

Institutional logics, as I understand them here, have a Janus-like character (after Janus, the two-faced Roman god of doorways, passages, frames, beginnings, and transitions). Institutional logics help us see the internal and lawful autonomy of overarching patterns of behaviours and describe the way in which different such patterns are reproduced and maintain their coherency. Logics are embodied in routines, systems, and rationales for action and in this way provide heuristics for action. An institutional logic is thus an ideal-type way of describing what is commonly or usually done in a situation. From the logic of patterns we have previously encountered, we can infer a solution (Jackall, 1988) that is characterized by appropriateness (March, 1994) rather than for example means–ends calculations; actors 'use criteria of similarity and congruence, rather than likelihood and value' as basis for action (March and Olsen, 2011, p 479). A simple example will illustrate this:

Coming into a café where people stand in line to order, you would most certainly queue up, too. When standing in line, you look at the menu and make a decision so that you can order swiftly when coming to the counter. Of course, it is not so that this happens automatically or that you necessarily do so – though other guests at the café might subtly (or even openly) show their discontent when you stand indecisively and fail to order within a reasonable time. It is also entirely possible to cut the line, or to run away with your latte without paying. Sanctions will likely be the response, but few actually calculate whether they will be able to get away with that latte without paying – it's something most people just don't do. If we view café-going from an institutional logics view, we could likely identify a number of rules, of which the actors are probably aware most. At least, if interrogated; most of the time we follow the logic unreflexively. Extraordinary situations bring the rules out into the light – when rules are challenged, we notice them (Garfinkel, 1967). The COVID-19 pandemic, for example, made us question and change the institutionalized rules for queuing. Suddenly, we found ourselves in a long line outside the café, queuing with two meters' distance and perhaps preferring a take-away coffee outside, despite cold winds and drizzling rain.

But, as I noted earlier, logics do not determine behaviour. There is room for mistakes, creativity, and overt rule-breaking. Challenging them might trigger responses that bring us back in line or may change the patterns of behaviour more or less permanently. Moreover, step-by-step changes barely noticeable to the actors take place, such as 'practical drift' when actual behaviour slowly starts deviating from formal procedure (Snook, 2000). At the level of action change, not stability, is the basic condition; stability and patterns must be maintained, intentionally or not (cf Latour, 1991). The view I take here thus allows for individual agency as well as unintentional 'drift', and thereby differs from, for example, Thornton et al (2012) who insist that agency mainly is a choice between different institutional logics. The role of agency is thus extremely restricted in their view (Alvehus and Hallonsten, forthcoming). However, if we stay *only* with a 'micro' view of institutional logics and the way in which they are followed, tweaked, and ignored in social situations, we will end up with a myopic view of organizations and behaviour. After all, we (or at least I) want to be able to address organizational phenomena and engage with both micro-sociological and macro-sociological issues (Barley, 2008; Gümüsay et al, 2020).

There is thus something more to collective patterns than the individual actions that comprise them. In the Janusian view I advocate here, the point is not to try to deduct or predict individual behaviour from general patterns that we can identify ideal-typically (institutional logics), nor is it a very good idea to view institutional logics as merely an aggregate of individual action. On a macro level I still want to talk about how different logics develop independently and seemingly without clear agency – their 'internal lawful autonomy'. On a micro level, I want to understand how actors' choices enact, transform, subvert, and ignore institutional logics.

3

The Ambiguity of Professional Service Work

In the first chapter, I argued for a view of professional service organizations where work takes the centre stage. In this chapter, I ask: How can we describe professional service work processes? What is it that is going on when lawyers, teachers, and physicians do what they do on a day-to-day basis? I take work processes as the starting point for my discussion but as I am interested in organizational questions, I will of course also, at the same time, discuss the organization of professional service work. My starting point is a common assumption about professional service work: that it is, by its nature, ambiguous, and that this inherent ambiguity has profound consequences for how professional service work is organized and managed. In the subsequent discussion I will problematize this assumption and suggest another view – that ambiguity is an outcome of the way in which professional service work is organized, just as much as it is a cause of it. A key theme running through the discussion is division of labour, and already at this point I want to emphasize that when I discuss division of labour in this chapter, I refer to 'detailed division of labour', that is, the division of labour taking place between workers, in practice, on an everyday basis. In discussions about professions, division of labour between different professions is often the topic (Freidson, 2001). We can of course also discuss division of labour at a societal level, for example in terms of gendered division of labour (a wonderful example is Gibson-Graham, 1996). Here, though, I am concerned with the detailed division of labour.

I will first start by accounting for the ambiguity assumption in professional work, and from this I continue with reflections over the way in which professionals talk about work. After this, I introduce different models for professional problem-solving, one traditional with 'cases' at the centre, and one with clients at the centre. Then, I discuss a common theme in discussions about professional service work: that it bears great resemblance to craft work and the ethos of craft work. Finally, I conclude with a discussion of the division of labour in professional service work.

Assumptions about ambiguity in knowledge work

The idea that certain types of work are by their nature ambiguous has become a key assumption in many studies of knowledge work. A classic statement foreboding this is Ouchi (1979), who argued that work can be directly controlled by either knowing and controlling the production process or by measuring its output. When we can create knowledge about the production process, we can prescribe in detail how to do the job. Following prescriptions will deliver consistency in quality and cost. This is the idea with industrial mass production. In some instances, however, we cannot easily describe the production process in detail. Instead, we might be able to measure output. If this can be done satisfactorily in terms of quantity and quality, we need not concern ourselves with the process. As long as we measure the output in relevant dimensions, this is enough to ensure that we get what we want.

But when we cannot control process or output – when these are ambiguous – organizations have to fall back on controlling the workers themselves. This can be done by formal training, by informal socialization, and by similar control mechanisms directed at the worker; Ouchi called it 'clan control'. This is, largely, the argument for why professional work – presumably by its nature hard to describe in detail, and difficult to measure in terms of output – leads to professional service organizations primarily relying on informal control mechanisms (I will discuss control in more detail in Chapter 4).

This line of argument is perhaps most clearly spelled out in Alvesson's seminal article 'Knowledge work: Ambiguity, image and identity' (2001), where he argued that knowledge work is inherently ambiguous, and that this in turn creates a pressure on organizations and professionals resulting in management being primarily directed towards identity and image. There are three ambiguities, he argues: in what knowledge actually is; in what knowledge workers do; and in how to evaluate the outcomes of knowledge work. All three ambiguities push knowledge-intensive firms towards emphasizing image (to appear professional), towards rhetorical claims to knowledge intensity, and towards working with social relationships with other organizations providing legitimacy (such as universities) and with clients. Alvesson's approach therefore serves as a powerful problematization of the claims to expertise made by professionals and knowledge workers. Undoubtedly this has been a key insight into the way in which professional work is undertaken, and in particular it brings the asymmetrical relation between alleged expertise and laypersons into the light (Sharma, 1997).

Ambiguity is something that skilled knowledge workers can use to their advantage, as they can exploit clients' lack of knowledge.

The core of professional work has accordingly been described as ambiguous, 'obscure', or 'hidden' (Clark, 1995; Power, 1997; Deetz, 1998), involving 'multiple meanings' and 'uncertainty that cannot be resolved or reconciled' (Alvesson, 2004, p 48). Professional work is primarily seen as a performance signalling knowledge intensity:

> when a magician pulls something from a hat it does not matter whether it is a scarf, a bird, a dove or something else. The role of these props is to support and sustain the magician's actions, which comprise the overall performance. Similarly, a consultancy report, the candidate shortlist and the results from psychometric tests all have relevance in that they assist the consultant both to maintain and to realize a performance. (Clark, 1995, p 127)

Undoubtedly this 'performance' view has had great value to the study of knowledge-intensive and professional work. Yet, it leaves things unsaid. The approach directs the gaze away from what lies behind the rhetoric and imagery, and towards how the imagery is accomplished. But the magician's hat must be constructed, the dove hidden, the scarves tucked away. In short, a good performance demands preparation, and this is what enables the performance in the first place. The problem, then, with stopping at saying that professional work is characterized by ambiguity, is that the details of why this ambiguity appears remain ambiguous.

The vagueness of professionals' talk

Perhaps the reason why the assumption of ambiguity is so persistent can be found in the way in which professionals themselves describe their work?

> There is a kind of magic to what we do with our clients. I can't really describe it to you. I certainly can't write it down on a piece of paper. (A management consultant in Morris and Empson, 1998, p 619)

> It's almost like painting. I can't tell you about it but I know it's like that. There's nothing supporting you, you have only yourself. You must find your way on dark and dusky roads. You create something together with that other person. It's a process – movement. And art is about movement. (A psychologist in Svensson and Östnäs, 1990, p 133, my translation)

It's almost been a taboo for some time, talking with someone else about how to do things. (A teacher in Alvehus et al, 2019b, p 143, my translation)

Magic. Art. By themselves somewhat mystical and vague terms. And a taboo about being explicit about each other's work; more vagueness. Of course, there might be other ways of talking about these types of work, but according to my own experience from interviewing for example teachers, consultants, lawyers, and accountants, these kinds of vocabularies tend to appear. It almost seems like professionals lack a clear vocabulary to describe what they do; much is taken for granted and never really explicated.

I do speculate a bit here, but perhaps the view among scholars that professional work is ambiguous is largely a matter of the consequence of a heavy reliance on interviews as a method for studying professional service organizations. Professionals are not used to explicating what they do to 'outsiders' – from a professionalism logic, outsiders cannot relate to the intricacies of professional work anyway. A case in point would be an interview I did with a tax lawyer. After the interview was finished, I asked if I could do observations of him working. He told me it was totally pointless, but that 'yeah sure, you can sit there and watch while I sort my papers'. And then he set about sorting the case files and at the same time he started talking about them, describing why some of the cases would go to very junior employees, why some of them would be necessary for himself to look into, why a certain individual was not quite suited to a certain task, why a certain client needed special treatment, and so on. From what he told me, I got a glimpse into what his priorities looked like and how cases trickled through the firm hierarchy – and thus a valuable insight into the way in which work was organized. Apparently not something worth talking about, in his view. (Different professionals, in this case lawyers and organization researchers, have different priorities and see different things as interesting.)

But, of course, he also had a point. Much professional work is of cognitive and interpersonal character, and is difficult to study with direct empirical methods. Gaining access to thought process is not easy, although there are methods such as elicitation[1] that could prove to be of some value (as my anecdote from the interview with the tax lawyer indicates). Moreover, much work happens in direct contact with clients, arenas where access may be difficult to negotiate for researchers. Still, client relationships are the part of

---

[1]   In elicitation, an interviewer uses a concrete artefact such as a photograph, an illustration, a text, a video sequence, or, as in this case, a pile of case folders, to trigger memories, associations, and lines of reasoning on behalf of the respondent.

professional work that has received the most attention among those interested in professional service organizations and knowledge-intensive work.

That we in general have only limited vocabularies for describing knowledge and work is sometimes explained by drawing on the notion of 'tacit knowledge' (Polanyi, 1966). The argument is that for example professional knowledge has a certain character, that it cannot be explicated, and this makes it different from other types of knowledge that can be. This is largely a misinterpretation of the original argument. Polanyi's point when introducing the term 'tacit knowledge' was that all knowledge has a tacit dimension. Thus the 'tacitness' is not something unique to professional or other forms of 'advanced' knowledge. Sandberg's (2000) study of engine optimization illustrates this very well.

Yet, this limited vocabulary in professionals' talk is interesting to interrogate further. It seems almost paradoxical. First, the way in which professional knowledge is about the application of formalized knowledge points towards large parts of the knowledge being explicitly accessible. Second, that language use is the foundation for many types of professional service work.

Professional expertise finds its legitimation in the close relationship with the profession's formal knowledge base: law, medicine, accounting, and so on. These comprise codified knowledge generally available, in for example books or scientific journals. Occupations having greater difficulties in establishing such clear knowledge bases – consider management consultancy, for example – find it harder to become recognized as professions. In general, professionals should be very skilled in talking about the knowledge base. But, professional work is about the application of knowledge, and the relationship with the formal knowledge base cannot become too unequivocal. If we all could successfully practice law after reading *Legalese for Dummies* we would not be inclined to hire expensive lawyers. The codified knowledge is only a part of the professional know-how, and at that, often the least crucial part. The know-how can only be gained from professional training and practice, and it is about craftsmanship rather than formal schooling, although schooling might be a prerequisite. A key part of professional training is to learn how to apply the abstract professional knowledge to concrete client situations. The application is what makes professional work unique, more so than the formal knowledge base. Thus, the explicit formal knowledge base will provide only elements of the real professional vocabulary.

Most professions are language based. In everyday professional work, a huge vocabulary is mobilized as part of the actual work and in coordination efforts. Some professions might be more solitary than others – the case-sorting lawyer earlier is one example of this. Others demand constant coordination, such as teams in teaching or accounting. In professional training, talk is arguably a key aspect of work. In becoming a physician, you will talk to other physicians about patients, lawyers talk about clients and developments in legislation, and so on. Yet most would probably agree that while talk about work, and reflection in action, might be key, this talk is not enough to describe what it is that is going on. Professional work is very much about doing, and talking about doing only gets you that far. If, indeed, a description of the work process would enable someone to follow it step by step and thereby be able to perform the task, it would be difficult for a profession to retain its status as this would be all too easy to copy (*Legalese for Dummies*, again). Sceptics have, accordingly, pointed out that this is why professions mystify what they do (Larson, 1977).

The question of what professionals actually do is thus left with only half an answer. Despite formalized knowledge base and everyday work being largely about language, the vagueness seems to prevail. But, if we try to gaze behind the vagueness of professional talk, what do we see? Are there other answers? One potential answer is that professionals solve complex problems. That is the reason we seek professional help in the first place, isn't it?

Working with cases: a model of professional problem solving

> The tasks of professions are human problems amenable to expert service.
>
> Abbott, 1988, p 35

Professional work is, as noted by Abbott, service work oriented towards solving client problems. (This was also part of the definition of a professional service organization I discussed in Chapter 2.) Sometimes, the problems solved are very unique to a certain client; other types of problem solving are fairly standardized and routine, such as much medical work. Furthermore, the way in which the client comes into the picture varies. Sometimes there will be a very strong orientation to interpersonal relationships (psychotherapy), sometimes the relationships comprise complexly intertwined organizational structures (large firm auditing). Sometimes, the relationship is little more than a handshake with the surgeon before the anaesthetic kicks in. Thus, there is a great deal of variety between different professions in terms of the characteristics of the problems they deal with, and how they deal with them. But in order to understand these characteristics we need a framework, and I will here follow Abbott's (1988) idea that professional problem solving is grounded in three distinct parts: 'to classify a problem, to reason about it, and to take action on it: in more formal terms, to diagnose, to infer, and to treat' (Abbott, 1988, p 40).

In *diagnosis*, the client's problem is brought under the light of the professional's knowledge system. In interacting with the client, the professional digs out the information that is necessary from the standpoint of the professional knowledge system. If you have a problem with stress at work, the information that will be produced by an organizational psychologist, a cognitive behaviour therapist, and a psychiatrist will likely differ. In a city planning project, the questions asked by landscape architects, environmental experts, and financial advisors will differ. Through interaction with the client, the professional starts to assemble a 'case', an abstraction representing the relevant information to the professional – from the perspective of their profession. This also means that information that is not relevant to the professional problem solving, from that profession's point of view, is excluded. For example, a surgeon will likely have little to no interest in your recent divorce, whereas this will be of great interest to your psychotherapist. A city planner might worry about how a new railway tunnel will affect the social sustainability of the city and look for information about this, whereas the engineer will care more about the properties of the bedrock and how to make the tunnel safe from the minor earthquakes that sometimes affect the area.

Diagnostic systems are often incredibly complex, and they only partly follow the clear patterns set out in formalizations of the knowledge system (such as those done by academics). The actual practice of diagnosis is learnt by interaction with other professionals and by developing personal experience – learning by doing. There will be ambiguities and difficult calls for judgement, but 'the ambiguity will be profession-relevant ambiguity—ambiguity within the professional knowledge system' (Abbott, 1988, p 41). This might go against claims of certain professions that they indeed take the client's whole situation into consideration; a 'holistic' view. I have for example when interviewing teachers come across such claims. Yet, these teachers do not engage in, for example, DNA screening. I do not suggest that they *should*, but they potentially *could*. Such tools and technologies are not part of the teachers' knowledge system in contemporary Sweden. Any knowledge system is always, by necessity, limited. In the professional problem solving, it is profession-relevant cases based on necessarily selective information that get constructed in the diagnostic process.

The case-model for professional problem solving is also practised at university. It is not uncommon for aspiring professionals to take part in case-solving activities where they learn how to apply the theories and methods they have learned to stylized cases that are presented as representative and signalling authenticity. In this, the students will also learn what information it is that is relevant, either by some information being presented and some not (and thus by implication not relevant for providing a solution), or by some information being mischievously inserted into the case as false leads.

Diagnosing and constructing a case is not enough, however. The diagnosis must be met with an adequate *treatment*. The treatment system available to a profession will mirror the diagnostic system, in that they deal with the same kind of problem and is based on the same knowledge base. It is not a simple one-to-one match-up, though. Some treatments might correspond to several diagnoses, and sometimes one diagnosis can be met by several treatments. Also, when administering the treatment, client-specific information will once again be brought into the situation, as client idiosyncrasies or demands come into play. A solution to a tax problem might be optimal from a financial and legal point of view, but the client might have other ideas, for example about risk exposure, that come into play. Again, this will depend on the profession at hand. Clients might be more inclined to push boundaries and expose themselves to risks in tax planning than in cancer treatment.

Making the connection between diagnosis and treatment is the act of *inference*, 'a purely professional act' (Abbott, 1988, p 40). In most cases, the specific connection between a diagnosis and a treatment will call for professional judgement. In fact, if connections between diagnosis and treatments become too routinized and too standardized, a profession risks losing its jurisdictional claim, as suddenly non-professionals will be just as able to make the call.

The way in which inference works varies according to the kind of problem that the profession deals with. In some professions, you get one chance only. Here, it is crucial to work out all potential logical steps in advance and ensure that the inference between diagnosis and treatment is optimal in order to ensure success. The consequences of failure are too dire. Other professions can adjust and adapt their solutions to a particular problem over time, trying out which treatment works best. In such instances, the stakes are lower in each step and a trial-and-error (or trial-and-success) approach can be applied. Interestingly, such professions will generate more failures in the process and they are therefore, Abbott (1988) notes, more susceptible to challenges from other occupational groups.

The diagnosis–inference–treatment model is quite schematic, however. What does it actually look like when professionals engage in problem solving? In *The Reflective Practitioner*, Schön (1983) draws attention to how concrete problem-solving situations are structured in everyday professional work. His argument is in line with Abbott's in that problem solving cannot be reduced to simple implementations of treatments to unambiguous problems. Schön suggests the concept of reflection-in-action to describe how professional problem solving takes place: a constant process of problem solving and problem definition while doing. Interaction between people and materials is central.

For example, he draws attention to professional learning situations. The problem-solving process as played out between teacher and student is about continuously probing and tweaking both problems and solutions. In one of Schön's examples, an architect, Quist, helps a student to develop a design of an elementary school. In the conversation, and by sketching and drawing ...

> Quist designs by spinning out a web of moves, consequences, implications, appreciations, and further moves.
>
> Once the smaller classrooms units have been made into L-shaped aggregates, they are 'more satisfactory in scale,' 'put grade one next to grade two,' and imply ('generate') a 'geometry of parallels in this direction.' Given these changes, Quist invents a new move: 'that being the gully and that the hill, that could then be the bridge.' The bridge also generates something new, an upper level which 'could drop down two ways.'
>
> Each move is a local experiment which contributes to the global experiment of reframing the problem. (Schön, 1983, p 94)

Small experiments are put into a larger whole, and the process is a search for a solution that works. In this, the architect student, Petra, and Quist constantly interact and try out ideas. Quist helps Petra reframe her problem and can thereby present a solution. Perhaps, then, the problem solving for the professionals (and soon-to-be professionals) is not as ambiguous as sometimes stated. The ambiguity confronting the professional is profession-relevant (as Abbott indicated) and this also means that it is ambiguity that can largely be resolved. Other ambiguities will not be part of the case with which the professional works. Whereas Quist might lack a distinct vocabulary for talking about how he accomplishes this with Petra, mirroring the vagueness of professional talk I mentioned initially in this chapter, this does not mean that he and Petra cannot accomplish it, or that it is too ambiguous. What Petra and Quist engage in is reflection-in-action, not reflection about action.

This account must not lead to the conclusion that all professional problem solving involves high degrees of ambiguity. As Abbott (1988) acknowledges, large parts of professional inference is routinized and professionals over time develop a repertoire of standard solutions. Sometimes these are also codified, as in in standard procedures for medicine. Too much routinization will threaten the professions' claim to knowledge intensity, too little routinization will be inefficient. Plastering tibia fractures at a ski resort will be very routinized, yet every once in a while, a complex case demanding extra attention comes in, where the professional judgement of not referring it to standard procedure is of paramount importance.

This account for professional problem solving still lies within Abbott's notion of inference. It is a question of profession-relevant cases, not clients. But this is a simplification that can only be made in a few instances. Abbott's model is, as much reasoning in studies of professions more generally, based on the medical profession in a US context. This presents a problem, since there are great variations as to how professionalism has panned out in different professions in different parts of the world, even within the rather limited population of Western industrialized nations. Possibly, the heavy reliance of the medical profession in the sociology of professions plays a part in the schematic models of professional problem solving. In other contexts, it is more difficult to remove the client from inference work. In those contexts the client gains a prominent role.

Working with clients: another model of professional problem solving

For someone who has followed the discussions on professional service work during the last 30 or so years, Abbott's view of professional problem solving comes through as somewhat archaic. The trend in private enterprises and public sector alike has been towards greater client and customer orientation. The cliché that the customer must come first has arguably become a cornerstone in the way in which we expect professional services to work. Also, an increasingly well-informed clientele will be more likely to challenge professionals in their suggested treatments. The central role of clients and client-related work has become a common theme in studies of professional service organizations. Research has highlighted, for example, whether relationships are relational or transactional in character, how client relationships are formed and developed, the consequences for knowledge development and strategy. (For an overview, see Broschak, 2015.)

But in the model of professional problem solving, the client is at the periphery, and progression within a profession takes the professional further from the client and towards the core – where the professional deals with cases, not clients. The most prestigious professional positions are, in Abbott's model, those most withdrawn from client interaction. In ideal-type professionalism, clients have little say. The reason we call on professionals is that there is a knowledge asymmetry, and the clients are ill-suited make diagnoses and infer treatments. This asymmetry can of course lead to arrogance and lack of attention to clients, their anxieties and their overall life situations – they become reduced to cases, and experience the situation as such. The platitude 'take two of these and call me in the morning' is telling, and criticism towards professions in, for example, public health care has been based on this lack of attention to clients as whole human beings. But it is important to differentiate between the role of expertise and the way in which clients and professionals differ in their relation to this, and blunt arrogance (as in the platitude just mentioned).

In a way, the client has always been important in professional work (also according to Abbott's model), and underlying the traditional idea of professional problem solving lies an assumption that the client's interest converges with that of the profession's (Bourgeault et al, 2011). A principal idea in traditional accounts of professionalism is that the client doesn't know what they want, or that they do not know how to express it. Sometimes, the value of professional work is not about clients at all – some professional work is forced on the client (as in parts of the legal and penal system).

There is a clear difference between a professional interested in doing what is best for the client and perhaps society, and a professional oriented towards what the client wants. Ideal-typically, returning to Freidson's typology (2001), this indicates a shift from professionalism to market-orientation. It is, however, not only a case of 'raw capitalism' forcing its way into professional services. We also need to understand this in relation to a backdrop of changes such as a clientele that is more well-educated and that has better access to information, more demands for accountability on behalf of professionals, ideas about 'user value' and 'value co-creation' (Skålén, 2018), and the introduction of market-like mechanisms in the public sector with the rise of New Public Management. In the context of professional service organizations this is often discussed in terms of an increasing marketization or commercialization (I will return to this in Chapter 8). In relation to this I think there are reasons to talk about a shift in the way in which professional problem solving works – perhaps we need to shift our understanding of what is at the heart of professional problem solving?

In Alvehus (2017, p 423) I argued for taking an 'inverted core-periphery relationship' in professional work into account. In studying the work of tax consultants, I discovered that senior and junior consultants seemed to confront very different ambiguities in their everyday work – they struggled with different types of problem solving. This we could expect from Abbott's model, as senior professionals will be working with the 'purely professional act' of inference, and junior professionals work closer to the client. What I found, however, was the opposite: seniors were mainly dealing with client problems, and juniors were handling much of the actual tax advice, that is, the inference work.

In terms of ambiguity, tax consultancy work involved inherent ambiguities. Tax law was (and is) continuously changing, and there was a constant stream of new court rulings and precedents. Sometimes whether a certain way of dealing with a transaction worked or not was a question that would only be known later, after court rulings and appeals. What constituted a smart, safe, and cheap solution for the client was difficult to know, and one consultant noted that tax law is so complicated that it was often 'more luck than skill'; another argued that sometimes 'you just have to not try to get everything a hundred per cent right, because it takes too much time and too much effort' (Alvehus, 2017, p 415).

Senior tax consultants described their work as mainly focusing on client relations. Part of this was social activities such as dinners or games of golf, where client relationships were created and reinforced. The more significant part however, as far as the core professional work was concerned, was understanding the business situation of the clients. The consultants worked closely with the clients, asked questions about future plans and mapped out the tax-related consequences of business decisions. One example mentioned was how to work out succession and ownership in family-owned businesses, another the strategic business consequences of offshoring solutions in tax havens. A key concern was understanding, and communicating with the client about, the risk exposure of different solutions. The tax consultants prided themselves with providing 'safe' solutions, yet the clients had different preferences and often needed to be held back from straying too far into the grey areas of tax legislation. Engaging with the client in order to develop solutions to their practical problem that fit each client's situation was key.

Junior consultants confronted a different set of issues. They were partly concerned with ethics, and struggled to cope with leaving the 'stick to the safe side' approach to legislation taught at law school. Much of their work was about getting a client folder and drawing up the legal solution to the problem as given to them by the senior consultant who had the direct client contact. They might get one of the folders sorted by the tax lawyer I mentioned earlier, and be requested to develop a solution and write a memo. In this, they felt they got very little guidance. In the firm this 'learning by doing' aspect was strongly emphasized, and feedback was often vague, and varied depending on which senior one was working for:

> You don't get that feedback concretely, explicitly; it's up to you to interpret the changes they've made to your drafts ... 'Here's what you wrote and that's generally good, but change this and that' or 'No, we have to structure this differently, turn it around'. Then you have to start all over again. (A tax consultant in Alvehus, 2017, p 416)

Client relationships were 'owned' by certain individuals. In comparison to accounting and auditing work in the same firm, tax consultancy was quite solitary and highly autonomous 'no one can come and tell me what I can do with my client' (Alvehus, 2017, p 418). Junior consultants were consciously kept outside client relationships: Their names were deleted from memos, the senior consultants shifted the juniors around so that the clients did not get to know them, and so on. It was therefore difficult for the junior consultants to develop the skills necessary for engaging with clients. Their ability to take initiative in this regard became a kind of litmus test – if one does not have the 'drive' and commitment to do this, one is perhaps not the right person for the job in the long run. It also became a question of developing the right relations with the senior consultants in the firm in order to gain their confidence.

Partly, this plays into the financial logic of commercial professional service organizations (see Chapter 4). It also, however, illustrates the way in which different ambiguities enter the professional work process, and how such ambiguities are actively maintained by the way in which work is organized. The profession-relevant ambiguity for the juniors was case-related and mainly concerned inference, whereas the profession-relevant ambiguity for the senior consultants was related to clients and mainly concerned diagnosis and solutions (treatment).

In the study of an accounting firm, Kornberger et al (2011) make observations similar to those I have made. There is, they argued, an 'organizational space between trainees and partners' (p 514) in such firms, that can be characterized as a *rite de passage* – a symbolic transitional stage between two groups, a changing of belonging and in identity. In their case this was about going from being a trainee to becoming partner. The title of their paper is telling: 'When you make manager, we put a big mountain in front of you', meaning that in these organizations, there are quite deliberate ways of testing the junior professionals before allowing them to make the final step towards becoming a partner. And again, it is not the technical inference skills that are at the centre. They argued that

> professional know-how provided a rather limited repertoire to deal with the complexities, ambiguities, and unpredictable contingencies that occurred in the network: technical expertise will get you only that far, to use the words of one of our interviewees … This begs the question: what knowledge did our managers draw on when they reflected about their practice? (Kornberger et al, 2011, p 531)

The knowledge that was relevant was relational knowledge: networking among clients and partners and 'interpreting rules of the game' (Kornberger et al, 2011, p 532) were necessary skills. In a similar vein – and in a similar empirical context – Dirsmith et al (1997) discuss how practices such as mentoring help junior professionals develop these subtle skills, far outside the formal knowledge of the profession.

In relation to Abbott (1988), then, we find a clear difference in these studies. The purely professional act of inference is what the junior consultants are confronted with, whereas the seniors' work largely concerns diagnosis and treatment – adapting the professional problem solving to clients. This does not mean that they do not engage in inference work, but it is often delegated and generally there does not seem to be very much ambiguity involved in it. I suggest that Abbott's model, with inference at the core and diagnosis and treatment at the periphery, is not the only way to describe the professional work process. In fact, I would wager that Abbott's model is primarily relevant to some of the medical professions (although admittedly this is mainly a hunch, and it would deserve thorough investigation). Moreover, it seems that the developments in professional service organizations over the last decades have tilted towards a client-centred mode of problem solving.

This will likely also entail shifts in terms of how we understand the power of clients. Often in the literature on professional services, clients are seen as rather powerless, perhaps due to the assumption of knowledge asymmetry (Sharma, 1997). However, clients are not passive. Instead they should be understood as active agents in the professional service work (Bourgeault et al, 2011) and professional–client relationships should be understood through a power lens (Sturdy, 1997; Sturdy and Wright, 2011). Recent trends in the field of public service management also emphasize the active role of clients in co-constructing value (Skålén, 2018), which have led some researchers to explore different ways of value-creation in for example health care (Stabell and Fjeldstad, 1998; Gadolin et al, 2020). Exploring this is however beyond the scope of this book.

In trying to understand the dynamics and division of labour in professional service work, we need to talk about two – ideal-typical, of course – different modes of professional problem solving: case-centred and client-centred. What is front stage and what is back stage – returning to Clark's (1995) magician analogy – differs between them. We can also expect professional progression and division of labour to differ. The becoming professional will start with different types of tasks, and gravitate towards different kinds of centres, in the two models. Yet, there are structural similarities here in terms of a systematic division of labour. In order to explore the precise workings of this division of labour, I want to draw in one more aspect: the imagery of craft work.

Professional work and craft work

In the beginning of this chapter, when I described the way in which professionals talk about their work, I left one aspect out: the notion of a craft. If you ask a professional worker to describe their work, there is a good chance that they will say that it is a craft, often implying that it is something that you learn by doing; that it about personal development as well as an effort to accomplish a product or service; that it strives towards mastership; that it is a way of life where work and non-work blend into a coherent, if sometimes conflicting, whole; that it is ultimately a question of satisfaction and pride in doing a good job. The origins of this professional ideal can be traced back to images of craft work. This makes sense, as modern-day professions have their predecessors in pre-industrial craft guilds (Krause, 1996) and there are many similarities between craft work and professional work. Ideal-typically, we can characterize craft work like this:

> work in which the worker produces an entire product ... where the worker's pace, workplace conditions, product, its use, and even to a degree price, are largely determined by the worker; where the source of income is a more individually-regulated sale of a product or service under fairly loose market conditions established by face-to-face bargaining, rather than sale of labour time (in advance of the creation of anything); and where virtually the whole income goes directly to the worker without any bureaucratic intermediary except perhaps an agent (as in the case of an artist). (Oppenheimer, 1972, pp 213–214)

Oppenheimer argued that this craft work image is mirrored in professionalism. And largely, this seems correct; compare this to the characterization of professional work in Chapter 1. However, this image of solitary craft work is only part of the story. Craft work has traditionally been fairly systematically organized and often performed in group settings, although not under the auspices of large bureaucracies.

The organization of craft work is built on a division of labour between master craftspersons and apprentices. In a traditional craft, the apprentice initially takes on simple tasks, such as running errands for the master. Yet by constantly being in the presence of the master, the apprentice gets glimpses of what a fully-fledged craftsperson does. Increasingly the apprentice gets involved in the craft, step by step moving towards more advanced tasks. This does not only concern the core production process; the apprentice also learns how the master cooperates with others, handles conflicts, manages customers, evaluates work, and so on. The apprentice learns not only a craft, but a way of life. This process is called legitimate peripheral participation (Lave and Wenger, 1991). For this process to work smoothly, transparency is 'a crucial resource for increasing participation' (Lave and Wenger, 1991, p 91) and when relationships work well they become 'privileged sites for a tight, effective loop of insight, problem identification, learning, and knowledge production' (Brown and Duguid, 2001, p 202).

The step between craft work and modern professional service organizations might, in the view of some, not be a very long one:

> The consulting firm may be viewed as the modern embodiment of the medieval craftsman's shop, with its apprentices, journeymen, and master craftsmen. The early years of an individual's association with a consulting firm are, indeed, usually viewed as an apprenticeship, and the relation between juniors and seniors the same: The senior craftsmen repay the hard work and assistance of the juniors by teaching them their craft. (Maister, 2004, p 17)

The image seems a bit romantic. It is as though physicians were still solo practitioners visiting middle-class homes with a doctor's bag, with an apprentice following along; but in fact, most are not. Instead, their job is often highly specialized and many work in large bureaucracies. Or accountants, who 80 years ago might have mainly worked in small firms with the name of the still active founders painted on the glass door to the office; today, four firms dominate the international market and each employ over a quarter of a million accountants. With size comes demand for organizing work and with this, among other things, a systematic division of labour. Yet there is a point to the analogy. Professional problem solving – both case-centred and client-centred – involves a journey from simpler tasks to more complex, similar to the one described in studies of traditional crafts.

During the apprenticeship, the apprentice provides simple labour at a low cost, partly repaid by allowing the apprentice to move from legitimate peripheral participation towards full participation and potentially becoming a journeyman and eventually a master. A benign analysis notes that the arrangement is to the mutual benefit of both: the master gets assistance and possibly a successor to carry her legacy. The apprentice has a job, learns a trade, and gets a future. A more critically oriented analysis would draw attention to the potential of exploitation and the dependence inherent in this asymmetrical power relationship: even if there are mutual benefits, the master controls and dominates the situation.

Craft work thus involves a clear division of labour but it also harbours an ideal of transparency, in turn often understood as key for efficiency. In a very concrete sense, for example by physical proximity in a workshop, the apprentices in Lave and Wenger's (1991) examples can observe the masters in action. It seems similar to the training of professionals described by Schön (1983), but far removed from the ownership of client relations in Alvehus (2017) and the mountains-to-be-climbed in Kornberger et al (2011). Ambiguity seems to still play a role in the professional division of labour; I will shortly return to this key part of my argument, after addressing the significance of ethics of craft work.

Professionalism and the craft ethos

With the imagery of professional work as craft work also comes a work ethic. In his exposé on the ethics and practices of craftsmanship, sociologist Richard Sennett argued that revitalizing the notion of craft might be a way of re-establishing the dignity of work, to regain the pride that is 'the reward for skill and commitment' (Sennett, 2008, p 294). Sennett's idea is to develop a vision of what craftsmanship can, or could, be. In this section, I follow Sennett's idea closely, but as this is largely an idealized image, we need to approach it with some caution. Just because something is labelled as craft work, does not automatically make it good.

To the craftsperson, 'the supreme concern, the whole attention, is with the quality of the product and the skill of its making', and other 'motives or results—money or reputation or salvation—are subordinate' (Mills, 1951/2002, p 220). This can seem somewhat romantic and archaic – but it is also something we can see traces of in professional codes of conduct and similar. The classic example would be the Hippocratic oath, which includes pledging to share knowledge, seeing the client (patient) as a whole human, admitting lack of knowledge, always working to the best of one's ability, understanding one's role in a broader societal context, and, of course, most known, not doing harm. Bowman argues for a professional ethos for public servants, claiming that the ethical concerns of modern public administration calls for a '*complete* professional [who] requires more than mere technical skill. He or she is not simply a professional because of expertise, but also because of adherence to high moral standards' (Bowman, 2000, p 676, emphasis in original). This is of particular concern not only because of the moral responsibilities that (should) come with the knowledge asymmetry in the professional–client relationship, but also because of the role that judgement plays in professional work. Schematically, in inference, matching diagnosis to treatment can never be a purely technical routine act. As put by Styhre, 'professional work cannot be fully captured by performance metrics and similar quanta because professional work always includes the capacity to cope with ambiguities and "weak signals" that is not apprehended by formal representations' (Styhre, 2013, p 183). This means that judgement is a key professional capacity involving making 'use of scientific knowledge under the influence of social demands and needs' (Styhre, 2013, p 198). Applying expert knowledge thus involves a broader set of concerns. This is, on the other hand, still cast under the limitations of the professional's knowledge base – as I argued earlier, professions deal with profession-relevant ambiguity and this has its limits. But a professional ethos strives to lessen the myopic tendencies inherent in expertise by at least trying to put knowledge, clients' interests and the professions' moral obligations in the driving seat. The idea of prioritizing the client's interest is central in many discourses on professionalism (see, for example, Anderson-Gough et al, 2000), and ideals such as altruism are often embedded in both descriptions of professionalism and in professionals' self-image. Whether this is an anachronism slowly dissolving in the dual acid bath of market and bureaucratic logic, or if it can be saved and restored, is a question I will return to at the very end of this book.

Division of labour and ambiguity in professional work

That professional work is inherently and necessarily ambiguous is a common assumption in studies of professional service organizations and professional service work. It is also something that is very concretely manifest in the way in which professionals talk about their work. This character presumably leads professional service organizations to adopt certain forms of control – 'clan control' (Ouchi, 1979) and identity regulation (Alvesson, 2001, 2004). In this chapter, I have challenged this assumption. I suggest instead a view where ambiguity is primarily seen as an outcome of the way in which professional work is organized and that ambiguity is highly functional in professional service organizations.

At the heart of the professional problem solving, we find profession-relevant ambiguity. In the transformation of clients to cases, many ambiguities are not dealt with – they are simply stripped away, and the remaining ambiguities are those that are manageable in relation to the profession's knowledge base. Learning how to deal with profession-specific ambiguity is systematically built into the professional division of labour, no matter whether clients or cases take centre stage. Of special interest, however, is the way in which ambiguity is managed within the professional division of labour. As the studies referred to earlier suggest, there is a clear parallel to be made with craft work, but it is a parallel that suggests a clear distinction.

In craft work, transparency is key for efficiency and learning. In professional work, however, ambiguity seems to play an analogous role. Ambiguities are created by the division of labour, and sometimes organized deliberately. It is by mastering ambiguities that the becoming professional proves herself worthy and able to deal autonomously with the profession-relevant ambiguity. Professional autonomy is something that must be conquered, it does not come automatically. The initial steps of training, where the aspiring professional deals with trivial tasks, serve a function. The process of becoming a professional is confusing and overwhelming. In this, reducing the ambiguity by piece by piece mastering the more mundane, routine, and standardized aspects of work can be beneficial initially. It helps learning key skills but also helps managing the situation per se. In a study of Portuguese lawyers, Santos notes: 'From the lawyer's perspective, standardisation is the beginning of a form of conquering autonomy, by knowing that she/he was taught in that manner and is precisely reproducing it, helping the lawyer to manage the anxiety associated to the new professional environment' (Santos, 2018, p 9). But mastering routine and standardized aspects only get you that far. It is in the light of this that we can see the significance and relevance of 'putting mountains' in front of people and excluding junior tax lawyers from client relationships. It might seem counter-productive and almost cruel if efficiency of learning is understood to be about transparency. But if we understand autonomously mastering ambiguity as a key element in professional work, we also see that the division of labour facilitates a gradual process in this regard, where the profession-relevant ambiguity shifts over time. Juniors face different ambiguities than seniors do. Ambiguity is built into the professional division of labour for a good reason – it facilitates the development of relevant skills, as they are precisely about mastering ambiguity. Too much transparency would be counter-productive.

There are three aspects to this that I want to highlight. First, there is clearly a division of labour between professionals within the same profession, that is partly opposite to the image of professional work as an autonomous and coherent whole. Second, the ambiguities in professional work are not only those inherent to the work. Quite on the contrary, the ambiguities in professional work are maintained through 'appropriate' (March, 1994) patterns of work, based on a division of labour. This opens up for exploitation of junior employees (and I will return to this in Chapter 4) but it also sheds new light on the way in which ambiguity plays a part in learning professional service work. Managing and navigating ambiguity is a core part of professional work and the learning of how to do so is an integrated element in the organization of the professional work process. Third, we may need to challenge Abbott's (1988) model of professional problem solving. We need to talk about two different modes of professional problem solving, one case-centred and one client-centred.

The relationship between ambiguity and the organization of professional work can thus be understood as comprising many different aspects of ambiguity rather than as a linear cause-and-effect relationship. Ambiguity seems to fulfil significant roles partly in relationships with clients (as observed by, for example, Clark, 1995; Alvesson, 2001) but even more so in that it maintains a division of labour within the professional service organization. This is in turn connected to the economies of the organization (see Chapter 4), and it also enables professional training and development. Ambiguity is beneficial, as it prepares the professional apprentice for dealing with profession-relevant ambiguity in the future. Being able to independently do this in turn facilitates autonomy.

4

Control, and Control over Control

Looking at the previous chapter, an almost paradoxical image appears. On the one hand, we tend to think about professional work as characterized by extensive individual autonomy, based on professional judgement, client-oriented, and difficult to evaluate. It is ambiguous to outsiders and organized to deal with profession-relevant ambiguity. In such circumstances it is of course difficult to exert control over the work process. On the other hand, there is a kind of management built into the professional division of labour, and professional socialization is in itself a form of control. In addition, most professionals work in large-scale bureaucracies and these are of course subject to various forms of control and management, as large-scale operations demand coordination efforts. As organizations grow, the need for bureaucracy develops, also in knowledge-intensive contexts (Mintzberg, 1979; Kärreman et al, 2002). All in all, professional service organizations are subject to various forms of management and control, formal and informal.

In this chapter, I will draw attention to some examples of formal control mechanisms in professional service organizations. The list is far from exhaustive, but it deals with two main dimensions of control (Ouchi, 1979): control over workers (here in terms of recruitment and career development), and control over work (here in terms of time and billable hours on the one hand, and quality and work processes on the other). After an initial point regarding terminology about bureaucracy, I start by addressing recruitment and career. Here, identity is a key theme. I then move on to discuss formal control systems, first in terms of how careers tie into up-or-out systems. Then, I take a closer look at the phenomenon of measuring time in terms of billable hours, and the next section also picks up on an aspect of formalization, now in terms of quality control systems and the role descriptions of work processes play. A recurring theme is how all these forms of control become transformed in organizational practice, and in the section on professional stratification I discuss the role that division of labour within a profession plays in such transformations. A fundamental insight in this chapter is how professionals often – not always – are able to take control over control systems, and with a discussion on this, the chapter closes.

A terminological warning

Partly the seeming paradox between autonomy and control I just mentioned comes from a confusion around what terms such as 'bureaucracy', 'control' and 'management' mean. If we look to the market–bureaucracy–profession typology (Freidson, 2001), it is all too easy to associate the notion of bureaucratic logic with a more general understanding of bureaucracy, management, and organizational control. The implication of a common-sense understanding of bureaucracy is that any efforts at controlling are instances of bureaucratic logic. But we must be careful here. Freidson's notion of bureaucratic logic is concerned with the question of with *whom* control over the work process ultimately resides, not whether forms of control and management are employed or not. It is not the case that professional logic lacks control procedures; professions and professionals are not unmanaged, even in the ideal type. Quite on the contrary. Professional logic implies internal management and control systems, for example mechanisms of exclusion, and meritocratic systems enabling professional progression. They are stratified, meaning that senior and junior professionals do somewhat different kinds of work (as discussed in Chapter 3), and that there is room for professional specialization, even towards managerial roles. In short, professions are organized (Freidson, 1985; Waring, 2014), and part of this organization happens by bureaucratic means (in a more generic, non-Freidsonian, sense). This does not mean that they are governed by a bureaucratic logic (in a Freidsonian sense). Indeed confusing – but mainly in terms of terminology. In this book, I use the terms 'management' and 'control' for describing practices in organizations and reserve the term 'bureaucracy' for when I talk about institutional logics.

Recruitment: the right person at the right place

Professional work is, at least traditionally, about something more than just a way of getting food on one's table. Being a professional is an identity, a way of being, a vocation. You do not *work as* a professional; you *are* a professional. Part of this somewhat romantic anachronism still holds true. As put by Maister (1993, p 185): 'Professionals want careers, not jobs.' This also means that recruitment to a professional service organization becomes a matter of finding those who want this career and thus a key element of control in professional service organizations is recruitment and development. Often this goes under the broad umbrella of human resource management (HRM; see Legge, 2005, for a comprehensive treatment of the concept). Indeed, in a context where the cliché 'the people are the most valuable resource' is actually relevant, it makes sense to manage these resources. I will zoom in on two key elements often associated with HRM: recruitment and career development, and the way in which professional service organizations by these aim to foster elite identities.

Starting chronologically, with recruitment, we can first note that this is partly something determined by the very notion of professionalism. Professions are (ideal-typically) tightly tied to university education, and the right university education is a prerequisite for most professions. This goes for medicine, law, accounting, and so on. This is not exclusive to professions, though, as many other occupations demand similar credentials. And in some cases, changes in professionals' work and the competence needed can lead to changes in educational demands.

Many professional service organizations – in particular in the commercial sector – strive not only to employ those with the right credentials, but the most prominent among them, for example by recruiting only students with high grades from high-ranked universities. This is of course no guarantee for competence or creativity – it is also about recruiting from certain social strata and about employer branding, being able to claim that 'we employ only the best and the brightest' and, thereby, if you get a job at such a firm you are evidently one of these bright people (cf Alvesson and Robertson, 2006). On an anecdotal level, I was told a story about physicians starting their education at Sweden's most prestigious hospital being introduced on their first day as being the most gifted students in the entire country, all categories considered. (Which incidentally is not entirely wrong, given the high demands for grades in order to make it into that particular education.) Already at that point, then, they are addressed not only as an elite in general but as the most prominent cognitive elite in the whole country; they have arrived at the *Top Gun* of medical schools.

Education, however, is not always enough. Professional service organizations often have more than credentials in mind when recruiting: they look for 'insecure overachievers'. Empson (2017) tells the story of an encounter with a director of human resources (HR) in a world-leading accounting firm:

> She explained the firm's policy of deliberately seeking out graduate recruits who fitted this profile [of insecure overachiever]. The firm looked for individuals with a track record of exceptional achievement on multiple dimensions throughout their school and university careers. She emphasized that, for these individuals to be suitable recruits, they

needed to be motivated by a profound sense of insecurity, which the firm could identify though psychometric tests and interviews. (Empson, 2017, p 109)

Never mind whether it is indeed possible to identify this 'personality type' – the ambition was clear. And this also goes for many other top-tier professional service organizations, Empson continues. Insecurity is key to exploitation: However hard the professional works, they are never sure it is hard enough. Could they do more? Better? The ambiguous character of professional work maintains this ambiguity in success. This can lead to self-imposed 'overwork' (Lupu and Empson, 2015) and drug abuse in order to keep up with the pace (Haight, 2001). Michel (2011) reports from a ten-year study of two US investment banks, where employees worked – purportedly voluntarily – up to 120 hours per week. Simultaneously they reported high degrees of autonomy and viewed the overwork as self-chosen. One banker said: 'I freely admit that I spend all of my time and energy at work. That's what I choose to do' (Michel, 2011, p 341). Yet, the socialization into this was organized through subtle control forms such as peer surveillance and facilitated through support structures (food, coffee, assistance with household chores). Over time, this put an extreme strain on their bodies and affected judgement and creativity.

Of course, not all professions – or occupational groups aspiring to professionalism – harbour such elite identities. High-school teachers may perhaps see themselves as of at least average or slightly above average intellectual capacity, but this does not amount to an elite identity. On the other hand, elite is a relative concept. Also, in schools there may be stratification between different professional workers and career stages. These are sometimes formalized, as in the Swedish notion of 'first teachers', presumably those teachers of unusually excellent quality suitable for a significant pay increase and other responsibilities such as 'pedagogical leadership' and 'collegial learning' (Alvehus et al, 2019a, 2020, 2021).

Career and professional progression

No matter if we look at the extreme example of investment banking or at the more mundane high-school teachers, a key feature of professionalism is progression, often taking the form of a *career*. Career is a way of making sense of one's professional progression – it 'links present, past and future through a series of stages, steps, or progressions' (Grey, 1994, p 481). Sometimes it involves fostering the kind of elite identities mentioned earlier, in other instances it is less dramatic and perhaps a more marginal phenomenon. It is nevertheless interesting as it ties into the notion of continuous learning and development, often understood as a core part of professional service work (see Chapter 1).

This also means that career is a strong control mechanism. Career, and the criteria for progression connected to it, is a way of directing the aspirations of the employees towards a goal that serves the organization. When formal systems for career and evaluation of progression have been studied, some scholars have argued that such systems shape the subjectivity of the employees. Career is seemingly a totalitarian machinery, and 'the status of the individual, that is, the individual's right to be different and everything that makes the individual truly individual tends to get lost in these processes' (Townley, 1993, p 537). Accusations that such systems turn employees into 'corporate clones' (Covaleski et al, 1998, p 300) have been made, and there is certainly some truth to this. At the same time, things are rarely that simple. There are intricate processes of interpretation going on when control systems are put into practice; I will get back to this topic later in this chapter.

Professionalism is not only about performing a number of tasks. Inhabiting a professional identity is also a question of behaving professionally. A study of a major accounting firm, for example, showed that professionalism was mainly seen in terms of 'appropriate forms of behaviour, or ways of conducting oneself, rather than with issues of accreditation to practice or the possession of "technical" skills' (Grey, 1998, p 569). This included language use, dress code, and managing issues of race and gender. The main focus seemed to be the front stage of professional work, not the back stage. And so, it mirrors the 'inverted' form of professional problem solving I discussed in Chapter 3, where the client, not the profession's knowledge base, is put at the centre of attention. Here, we can see the 'corporate clones' argument turning into a visual reality: 'a white heterosexual middle-class man' (Grey, 1998, p 584).

There is another and slightly more optimistic aspect to career, however. Remember the point made in Chapter 3, that the sole autonomous professional is a rather archaic idea? And that professional work instead should be understood as involving a division of labour? Let me delve a bit more into this.

Consider how physicians develop in their career. A physician in the UK, for example, starts off with a long university education, typically five years. This involves non-clinical education and clinical work. After this they enter a two-year foundational programme, where they encounter different specialties and obtain a broad understanding of different form of clinical work. After this, they go into training towards specialisms as specialty registrar leading on to general practitioner or a specialized consultant. All in all, the post-university training involves a series of steps on a career ladder and it takes about ten years.[1] Career progression in accounting or law follows similar patterns. With each step comes a series of rights and responsibilities. Of course, it can be argued that the steps are arbitrary, that the criteria for progression are sometimes not clear, and that an unreasonable emphasis is put on commercial and/or managerial activities. And, of course this cannot be reduced to a control process for ensuring that profession-relevant competence is established. As all such processes it will involve socialization and identity development. But when drawing on the example of physicians, the notion of career development seems somewhat less arbitrary and more relevant. It is a way of trying to ensure that clients are treated by competent professionals. It is less easy to shrug it off as merely a question of identity control and the production of 'clones'. Arguably then, in some cases there is a clear function to step-by-step progression patterns connected to a curriculum of professional development. Identity production will of course take place; it always does. To the extent that it fosters elitism and professional arrogance – the classic 'take two of these and call me in the morning' cliché again comes to mind – this can be a problem that should be dealt with. Yet the idea of progression and development is key to professionalism.

This understanding of progression also mirrors the professional division of labour. Moving from legitimate peripheral participation towards full participation is a process, and in this process junior professionals get increasingly wider responsibilities. In a medieval craft workshop, there might not be any need for formal step-by-step credentials as master and apprentice will be in a tight long-term relationship. But today professionals often work in large organizations and everyone cannot know everyone. Formalized systems of progression within the profession are a way of facilitating mobility. Career is a core part of many professional systems and therefore it is essentially a control mechanism that also serves the broader interests of the profession.

As an aside, many occupational groups with distinct identities are less concerned with career. This however seems detrimental to developing a distinct professional identity; later I will discuss the role that stratification plays in the control over professional work, which is in turn related to the career concept.

In many cases, career planning and HRM systems in professional service organizations emulate a professional logic of progression. Firms will often develop their own version of career steps and incentives, but the more formalized these are by professional bodies, the less space there is for deviance.

---

[1]   A special thank you to professor Justin Waring for conversations on this. See https:// en.wikipedia.org/wiki/Medical_education_in_the_United_Kingdom (accessed 20 January 2021).

Career systems are ways of circumscribing autonomy and directing the activities of aspiring professionals to certain ends. But the question is, of course, the ends of the profession or the ends of the employing organization?

> [T]he career plan establishes a relation of dependency, creating a different type of professional autonomy. What the lawyer will internalize is autonomy in a dependent relationship with the hierarchy of the firm and not in a collegial form, where all lawyers are autonomous on their practice and based their decision on their internalized knowledge of the profession. (Santos, 2018, p 10)

Today, dependency in many professional service organizations seems to move towards the organization instead of the profession (Evetts, 2011; Kirkpatrick and Noordegraaf, 2015) and while this might still maintain autonomy for the individual, it does not guarantee professional autonomy.

Thus, while the critique of shaping elite identities has its relevance, what needs to be recognized is that the key element is perhaps: to what ends? Professional logic and bureaucratic or market logics represent not the existence or non-existence of career systems. As noted at the beginning of this chapter, control is key also to professional logic. And what I am arguing is that there is a functionality to formalized systems of progression that can be useful for professionals and professions alike, just as they can be used in organizations aiming to establish elite identities.

Up-or-out systems and careers

A prime example of organization- or firm-oriented career systems are so-called up-or-out systems (Baden-Fuller and Bateson, 1990; Sherer, 1995). An up-or-out system is characterized by a pyramid structure, where workers are expected to move 'up' or, if they fail to perform according to criteria, move 'out' of the firm. At each higher level, there are fewer positions than in the previous one, effectively creating competition for upward movement. At the top is the promise of partnership, where one becomes an owner of the firm and shares profits. (This is a rough outline of the underlying logic, and there are variants of this; see Empson and Chapman, 2006.) As 'most professionals aspire to partnership' (Greenwood et al, 1990, p 731) the up-or-out structure effectively creates a fairly self-sustaining control system, where aspiring professionals will adhere to performance criteria for their own survival in the organization.

The pyramid structure makes some sense from a division of labour point of view. Each 'master' (that is, partner) has a number of people below to whom tasks can be delegated; each of these in turn a number of people below, and so on. The leverage achieved by this is the 'heart' of the financial logic of professional service firms (Maister, 1993, p 8) – and with the previous chapter in mind, we could add in that this is primarily the matter in client-centred division of labour. Senior professionals sell work to clients, maintain client relationships, and serve as guarantors of quality. The large share of inference work is done by junior employees, at a lower cost (Kor and Leblebici, 2005). In this way a surplus is generated to the firm (that is, the partners), as the client can be billed at full rate while the work is done at a lower rate. This is one way of leveraging human assets and creating surplus.

The problem is of course that the up-or-out system is based on growth, but it cannot grow infinitely. For each new partner, there has to be a new pyramid below to sustain that partner. Imagine a firm with five partners at the top and where each has five people below, and so on for all levels. The organization has five levels. Thus it comprises $5 + 5^2 + 5^3 + 5^4 + 5^5 = 3,905$ people. What happens if we expand by one partner? Or when everyone at the second level aspire to partnership? What happens if we try to delay expansion at the top by creating a new level just below partnership? Do the math, it is quite interesting! In an up-or-out system, each new partner needs to expand the business in order to avoid diluting profits. Thus, the rapidly expanding up-or-out system is essentially a Ponzi scheme as markets are limited (and this also partly explains why professional service firms often divest into new businesses). If expansion stops, the system will grind to a halt as the upward flow stops. It effectively becomes a 'dead man's shoes' system, where movement up is only triggered by people at the top leaving, creating a downward cascade. But this is a fairly weak system of incentives, as individual careers will entirely depend on people retiring. (See Baden-Fuller and Bateson, 1990, for more extensive discussions.)

The up-or-out system seems perhaps more relevant in relation to for-profit professional service firms. However, there are similar tendencies in, for example, universities today. Not so long ago in Sweden, there were a finite number of professors' chairs (new ones were rare), and commonly the way to get to hold such a chair was to wait for someone to leave (that is, retire or die). This also meant that ending one's career in a non-professor position would still be a reasonable achievement, as you might simply not have the 'fortune' of a chair becoming available. Again, then, a dead man's shoes system. (Often, quite literally – both in terms of 'dead' and 'man.') However, universities now have seen a value in the more 'efficient' incentive system of up-or-out, and in many instances becoming a professor depends not on being an accomplished scholar and having some luck in the succession game, but also – and increasingly, I would argue – on drawing in funding and producing high-status publications that, too, secure funding as they increase output and status. Increasingly professors need to be able to show that they can sustain their own chair and preferably obtain funding for new PhD students: growth as a value in itself, not dissimilar to an up-or-out firm. Those less accomplished in attracting funding might have a harsh future in the academic career system. This, in turn, erodes traditional academic values in terms of what it means to accomplish good research, and instead moves towards a market-like system (cf Tourish, 2019).

In client-centred professional service organizations, career systems are often tied to financial performance, according to the up-or-out logic. As noted, this is an efficient and affordable control system, as long as the performance criteria are relevant. And in a financialized system, relevant performance criteria are often just that: financial.

Accounting for time

Whereas the previous three sections (centred on recruitment and career) were concerned with the control of knowledge workers, this section and the next will focus on forms of control more directly engaged with work itself.

First out is time.

In my early days teaching at university, when I was doing my PhD, the yearly teaching curriculum for a full-time teacher was 400 'lecturing hours'. One hour in class – lecturing, running a seminar, or such – equalled one lecturing hour, thereby compensating for, for example, preparation time. Some years later, the system changed from lecturing hours to 'clock hours'. Four clock hours initially equalled one lecturing hour, making the yearly curriculum roughly the same: One hour in class lecturing ticked off four clock hours from the 1,700-hour pensum, and the change in teaching pensum was minor. However, soon after the change to clock hours, compensations started to diminish. Seminars went from being compensated with four hours to three and, a few years later, to two. The work input expected was the same. While traditional lectures were (and still are) on a 4:1 basis, average compensation became significantly lower due to seminars and other, less well-compensated, activities. The earlier system did not allow for this, and of course the system change did not necessitate it – but it was certainly facilitated. A drawback with the old system was of course that the incentives for change were low; on the other hand, compensation was generous enough to accommodate for updates and changes to lectures and seminars, and the incentive was rather tied to the professional ethos of the teacher. The new system has not created stronger incentives for change. (Or for anything else, for that matter. Yes, I'm slightly bitter.) In Marxian terms, a straightforward intensification of surplus value extraction occurred (for a detailed discussion of exploitation in higher education, see Curtis, 2001).

In the absence of a concrete product, time is often what professionals 'sell' – on a market or within an accounting system in the organization, as in my academic experiences. In commercial firms, a common practice is accounting for time in terms of 'billable' or 'chargeable' hours. This basically means keeping track of the hours that you work within a specific project or job and making sure that these are then billed to the right client. On the surface, this does not seem like a problematic practice. Keeping track of what one does, for which client – it should be fairly straightforward. However, this is not always the case.

The idea with accounting for time is that this is a way of representing work. Often the idea seems to be that the registering of billable hours operates in the background, as a clockwork. This of course neglects the way in which time is actually registered: through one or another form of self-monitoring. Someone (that is, the professional) has to enter the time worked into some sort of system. I myself have seen professionals working with an Excel spreadsheet constantly on screen, registering their time every six minutes (so that one hour becomes ten time slots). In itself an effort, but also a way of creating a constant awareness of the allocation of time and a sense of urgency.

One problem that immediately occurs is what work to register – what should be considered work? If you are working on a solution for a client, and it suddenly turns out that you have been on the wrong track for the last two hours: Where do you register this? There might be a 'null option', but do you *really* want to tell your manager that you are wasting company time doing things wrong? Those hours might simply not make their way into the system, and instead you have made your mistakes and presumably learnt something important for the job in your spare time. As expressed by a second-year associate in Santos (2018, p 11), 'studying is good, but it's not a billable hour'.

Alvehus and Spicer's (2012) study of an accounting firm describes this in detail. We argued that billable hours turned into a kind of game-playing. In the study reported, there was clearly talk about billable hours in a clockwork-like sense: 'what we make a living of is billing for our work. And work in consultancy is normally related to time, so to speak. That means that the utilization totally determines the survival of the firm' (a partner, in Alvehus and Spicer, 2012, p 501). In itself this produced a demand for continuous self-surveillance, with five-, six-, or ten-minute time slots to be continuously reported and at the end of the day summarized in a time report. The working day became quantified and 'employees are constantly forced to make judgements about what is valuable work by using the sole criterion of whether it might be charged to a client or not' (Alvehus and Spicer, 2012, p 502). Yet the key impact was the way in which the billable hours was turned into gameplay. This took place between people in different levels in the career hierarchy (beginning with assistant and then consultant, manager, and finally partner), and was described in elaborate detail by a consultant. First, he noted, seeking help from others was very expensive, and in practice this meant that they tried to obscure some of their work, in order to keep the billable hours for control down. Another option was to push the job downward in the organization to someone with less bargaining power:

> Take me for instance, I bill 1600 kronor [SEK] per hour, and we have a Manager, he bills let's say 2000 kronor. And you have a new Assistant who bills 900 kronor per hour. And you know that this job is worth 10 000 at a maximum. If you're going to do it yourself you quickly figure out that six hours, then you're at 9000 kronor, and a thousand for peer review, that doesn't work. 'Six hours, shit, I can't do this in six hours.' Then you ask, maybe, let's say Eve, and you say 'Hell, why don't you do this job Eve, you get four hours maximum, not more than four, maybe five.' You know what I'm getting at? You force her to do a job you should have done yourself, could have done, but in order to keep within the price, to avoid over-billing or not being able to get the client to pay, for instance, or in order to get some more time for yourself you squeeze someone else, push it down to some Assistant who can do it cheaper. And you can keep the margin for yourself, maybe review what she has done, and go below the 10 000. So you can bill 10 000 without having to go to a Manager. Or you spend a little time on it and when you come to the manager it's just for him to read through, 'yes it's ok,' it's a cheap way of dealing with it. This becomes a necessity because of the system itself. (Alvehus and Spicer, 2012, p 505)

Note how naturally the calculations come to the consultant; they are at the tip of his tongue. This is something routinely done, in efforts to maximize one's own billable time and in the process exploiting others. Those below you in the hierarchy are targets for exploitation and enable keeping your own work effort at bay, and those above you get as little information as possible in the review, so they don't charge too much – thus potentially impacting quality control (which was the point with the review system). Juniors on the receiving end of this know they will have to clench their hands in the proverbial pocket; the one that overcharges or does not accept the unpaid overtime will likely not get any more jobs and thereby pay the price in terms of lost career opportunities. This is explicitly acknowledged:

If someone calls you and, he's going to get on his report how much you bill, and he's going to bill the client, and if he calls me it costs 25 000 and if he calls Charlie it will cost 50 [000], I mean … And of course they take advantage of this. (Alvehus and Spicer, 2012, p 505)

The consultants in the firm needed to learn to see the 'lost' work as an investment in their own future. Thus, it is quite inconceivable to understand systems of billable hours as neutral clockworks, registering time in the background. It is not (merely) a surveillance system; it is also a way of creating a 'financialized' workplace where each worker turns into a quantified unit of performance (see also Cushen, 2013).

This financialization is not the only possible outcome, however. Time can also be an expression of loyalty. Alvesson and Kärreman (2004) report on the phenomenon of 'ghosting' from an international consultancy firm. There, the employees always reported an eight-hour working day when working in projects, despite the actual work time often being significantly higher. This was recognized as a problem by management and workers alike. It made it difficult to get proper data to predict actual costs on future projects, for example. However, ghosting enabled those working in projects to appear quite productive and therefore eligible candidates also for the next project – just as the junior professionals in the accounting firm in Alvehus and Spicer (2012), they had to sell themselves cheap. Also, the project managers were able to sustain high profit margins on their projects in the internal reporting system (although this had no effect on the real money in/money out for the firm). Thus, ghosting was a way of displaying loyalty. In a meeting where the ghosting was addressed, one employee said:

The whole thing depends upon the fact that there are no incentives to report the correct time. Who are you loyal to, really? … In the first place you are loyal to yourself. In the second place [you're] loyal to the project, and only in the third place are you loyal to the firm. (Alvesson and Kärreman, 2004, p 434)

The practice of recording billable hours is common in professional service organizations with a strong commercial orientation, and often the accumulation of billable hours is strongly tied to an up-or-out system. In other services, similar practices occur, such as in resource consultancy (for example, IT-system specialists for hire). In an extensive study of freelance technical contractors, Barley and Kunda (2004) show how they constantly need to make temporal trade-offs between work assignments, investing in training, and spending time with family and friends. All in all, a situation where there is certainly a degree of freedom, but at the same time the conditions of this freedom are dictated by the markets in which they operate. Elsewhere, as in my initial example from academic work, the situation is somewhat less tense (at least so far). Yet, also there we find wangling – people holding on to courses they have taught for a long time where their investment has already been made, the struggle for more 'lucrative' courses, and so on. (And I haven't even mentioned the struggles between departments for funds and how to assign costs to different student groups, thereby creating a budget for courses, and thereby in turn affecting the number of teaching hours available for allocation ...)

In other contexts, we will find other 'currencies' in play. Physicians are often measured by the number of patients they meet during the day; for teachers, the number of students that reach target grades might be measured, and so on. Different measurements will trigger different forms of game-playing, and this does of course not concern only professional service work (the classic example is Burawoy, 1979) but the general take-away is that control systems are never 'implemented' – they are transformed and translated (Czarniawska and Joerges, 1995), and in this process, the tweaking of the systems can easily undermine what the systems aimed to accomplish in the first place.

Controlling quality and process

Professional work is, in the ideal-type sense, difficult if not impossible for non-professionals to easily evaluate in terms of quality. This is the essence of the notion of knowledge asymmetry between the professional and the client, and is a justification for society to maintain professional monopolies, as long as the profession maintains self-regulation. If the quality of the services could be easily evaluated, we would not need to trust the professionals. But, taking the example of medicine:

> in the actual transaction itself, the patient faces the physician alone. The patient, therefore, must rely exclusively on his own uninformed judgment since, indeed, the information he has about the effectiveness of the services he is getting is always indirect or ex post facto: he can judge his doctor only through the subjective assessments and experience of other patients, through the realization that he is not getting any better (or that he is not improving fast enough), through non-functional factors of confidence, or through the judgment of other doctors. (Larson, 1977, p 22)

In ideal-type professionalism, quality is matter of judgement and subject to qualitative valuation that only professionals can do.

That is, however, not the reality in many professional contexts. Instead, efforts are often made to control, follow up, and evaluate the quality of the services provided. This might not always be such a bad idea – for example many of us appreciate that health care ensures that high-standard care is given, and measurements of such things as post-operative complications and effects of medication are all there for a good reason. On the other hand, the question of what constitutes 'good health care' remains unanswered, and there seems to be little that cannot be measured – 'staff sickness and absence levels, number of patients, ward/bed usage, healthcare acquired infections and complaints … month-on-month figures for patients treated, delays, cancellations, readmittance' (Waring and Bishop, 2013, p 150) – just for a start. The question of on what to focus remains, and so does the more tricky issue of interpreting what the measurables actually mean – again a question where ambiguity, and therefore professional judgement, comes into play.

Another example from university: course evaluations. There are many different things that can be measured when evaluating a university course. You can look at how many students pass the exam. Handing out surveys after courses is common practice, aiming to capture students' experiences. Sometimes student employability after finished education is measured. But none of these are unequivocally related to the quality of a course or university programme. Exams can be made easier in order to increase student throughput. Students might be feeling disappointed after a course and give it low ratings – but perhaps they would rate it higher once they saw the role of the course for later studies, or perhaps they had expectations of what the course would deliver that are simply not possible to live up to. And perhaps employability is not the only, or even the most, relevant way of measuring the value of a university education. All in all, these measurements might be only vaguely related to any substantial notion of quality, and in some instances even counter-productive.

Measuring quality in terms of outputs is difficult and sometimes misleading. Sometimes, keeping an eye on quality in quantitative and measurable, terms, is a way of ensuring that high standards are maintained, and it can also be a source to draw on in development work. Other times, resistance to implement such measurement is a way of defending a professional turf by maintaining a veil of mystery around what the professional work is about.

Control over work can however also be directed at the work process. Here, another challenge to the traditional image of professional work occurs. Is not professional work autonomous and undertaken at the discretion of the professional? One may wonder why this image still persists. In some cases it may still be relevant, but today, physicians, nurses, accountants, lawyers, and so on commonly work in teams. In auditing there are models that structure work, and would anyone want a surgical team that did not have any standard operating procedures? Such procedures are also under constant development. My favourite example is this: A team of physicians were invited by a Formula One racing team to observe its work in the pit stop. In a coordinated team effort, a pit stop team refuels and changes the tires of a racing car in approximately seven seconds.[2] In subsequent discussions, similarities with handovers between surgery and intensive care were explored. Then, drawing on the expertise of two training captains from aviation, they developed a new handover protocol involving clear division of roles, checklists, a formal structure for communication, and so on. By this – at least in the experiment – they significantly reduced risks in the very sensitive handover procedure. (See Catchpole et al, 2007.) Who knew that Formula One racing had something to offer beyond speed, fancy cars, and adrenaline!

In other cases, process descriptions and models are less significant in carrying out the work. In management consulting, models are common, for example models describing change processes. These models are often portrayed as vital or even revolutionary: following the prescriptions is the royal road to financial salvation. The models are often extremely structured and rational:

> They identify a number of steps in the change process – up to 67 [in one case]. Each step is described at least in terms of its purpose, content (what the consultant and the client should do) and results (documents, etc.). Often templates for analysis and checklists are provided to support the different steps. (Werr et al, 1997, p 299)

In parallel with these rational models, the significance of the management consultants' expertise and competence is emphasized. And, after all, there's a logic to this: If the models would work straight out of the box, the consultants would be redundant and this would not be good for business. In reality, then, the role of these models is more dubious. They rarely seem to be followed, and as so many studies of change processes show, organizational change is vastly more unpredictable than management models and popular management literature claim. To some extent, change models may have an internal function in management consultancy firms, in that they can play a part in the socialization of new recruits, and in making it easier to transfer people between projects. But the main role seems to be in convincing presumptive clients that the firm has something really well thought out to offer, and they mainly serve as a tool for communicating and sense-making and generating a convincing sales proposition. (As a sidenote, it is worth remembering that most sound advice for change management has been

---

[2]   At the time that the study was made. Judging from a quick YouTube search, it's now down to less than two seconds. Impressive!

pretty much the same since Coch and French's study of change in a pyjama factory in 1948.)

A final example is financial auditing. It needs to be practical and understandable enough to seem trustworthy to clients and stakeholders, for example in the models used to select specific transactions to be scrutinized, often including a risk assessment. However, a basic problem in auditing is that if an audit finds no faults – is this because there were none, or because none were discovered? Increasing assurance levels are associated with higher costs, but how this relation looks, is essentially impossible to know. This 'deep epistemological obscurity' (Power, 1997, p 28) causes auditing firms to invest large efforts in convincing formal procedures, codes of conduct and other forms of image work in order to produce credibility. The same of course applies to internal control systems.

It would be rather useless to continue listing different control forms. By now it should be clear that controlling quality and processes in professional services is complicated. The lesson to be learned is that it is never simply a matter of controls being straightforwardly implemented into the professional work process. Instead, we see that there are signs of struggle over the control over the work process. And, there is also struggle over controls themselves.

Professional stratification

Much of what I have discussed so far in this chapter relates to forms of control internal to a professional service organization. Yet, in many cases, there are forms of control emanating from outside the organization. Formally recognized professions will likely want to maintain systems of exclusion for malpractice, and perhaps make continuous training available to their members, both cutting across organizational boundaries. In other instances, there might be external interventions, such as legislation, that force professions to adapt.

Professions have a specific way of dealing with such imposed formalized control systems: professional stratification. Freidson describes it thus: 'elite members of the profession perform special roles in professional associations and institutions and engage in critical negotiations with legislators and government officials in shaping laws and administrative procedures as well as with the governing boards of hospitals and other institutions' (Freidson, 1985, p 22). Freidson's argument is mainly on a systemic level, and his idea that professions should be understood as systems has only recently gained traction in discussions on professional service organizations. But, in line with the overall argument of this book, we need to bring these overarching questions to the coalface of everyday work. For, as Freidson notes, stratification affects the everyday work of the 'rank and file' professional. It 'means that their discretion must take into account the authoritative norms laid down by other members of their profession, that they become in some sense subordinate to a select group of their own colleagues' (Freidson, 1985, p 29). Stratification thus means that the profession takes control over control. Let me illustrate how this can play out in everyday work by two examples, one from medicine, and one from schools.

In a study of Independent Sector Treatment Centres (ISTCs) in the UK, Waring and Bishop (2013) note that these care units work with comparatively high degrees of standardization. The ISTCs are intended to take some load off the National Health Service (NHS), increase patient choice, and reduce the waiting times; they typically 'undertake "bulk" surgery such as hip replacements, cataract operations or MRI scans rather than more complex operations'.[3] To some extent this standardization leads to 'McMedicine' (Waring and Bishop, 2013, p 153) where the professional judgement of individual doctors is underplayed and rank-and-file doctors become severely circumscribed. Yet at the same time, other doctors retained and even increased their power in the organization:

> Those doctors taking a more engaged approach to ISTC work were characterised by different structural resources. This relatively small group of doctors had higher levels of autonomy and scope to adapt ISTC procedures to reflect their preferred modes of working. These opportunities seemed to stem from their relatively unique contribution to the ISTCs in terms of specialised case mix and, in turn, financial value. As such, it seemed necessary for managers to accommodate these doctors rather than risk their exit from the service. (Waring and Bishop, 2013, p 153)

Thus, to some extent, the medical profession was able to take control of the processes of standardization, and the elite doctors 'were able to draw upon both economic and symbolic resources to advocate "new" ways of working' (p 154). In this they to some extent aligned with the commercial interests of the organization, yet they protected their professional turf, albeit by accommodating to new pressures.

Another study addressing similar issues is one I was part of, looking at Swedish teachers (Alvehus et al, 2019a, 2019b, 2020, 2021). In 2013, the Swedish government instituted a new position for teachers in schools, that of 'first teachers'. This was a response to the generally accepted view of a

---

[3] See https://en.wikipedia.org/wiki/Independent_sector_treatment_centre (accessed 25 March 2021).

long process of deprofessionalization among Swedish teachers. Appointment to the new position was made by school principals and was accompanied by a salary increase of 5,000 SEK for the teacher, at the time an over 15 per cent increase on an average secondary school teacher's salary.

However, this was not received very well. Swedish teachers are extremely egalitarian, even in a Swedish context. Some appointed first teachers even got ironic degrading nicknames such as Fürst Teacher.[4] Thus,

> the newly appointed [first teachers] had to find a way of establishing their new expert role in relation to other professionals in the school organization: in relation to the other teachers (intra-professionally) and to the principals (extra-professionally). As implementation was left up to local school organization, the specific and concrete effects of the reform were results of processes of negotiation and struggles in the workplace. (Alvehus et al, 2019a, p 35)

After a few years, while still not totally accepted in the everyday chit-chat in the senior common room, the first teachers became taken for granted, part of everyday school organization. They managed to expand the jurisdiction of the teachers, for example by first teachers becoming a part of school management teams and taking on responsibility for school development and pedagogical leadership. They were therefore able to appropriate key tasks from principals – in Sweden, principals are effectively a different profession – and expand their jurisdiction. However, the process was not similar in all instances. Different first teachers found different ways of relating to their new role. Some took on a strong role as collegial 'first leaders', other did not expand their jurisdiction and remained 'star players', focusing on teaching. Yet others became 'deputies' to their principals, and thereby related more strongly to them than to their default identity. All in all, the reform led to a subtle yet significant reorganization of tasks and jurisdictions in the school system, and in contrast to the hybridized role of the elite doctors in the previous example, the first teachers seem to have 'de-hybridized' and split into even more different roles.

Returning to the overall question of the role of stratification, we might ask: Were the elite ISTC doctors part of creating a pseudo-professionalism subjected to the organization's bureaucratic logic (Evetts, 2006, 2011), or was it an opportunity for the profession to draw on the new system in order to

---

[4] Incidentally this play with words works in English as well as in Swedish; first teacher/ fürst teacher versus förstelärare/furstelärare. 'Lärare' means teacher, 'förste' means first, and 'furste' can be translated as fürst.

build legitimacy (Kirkpatrick and Noordegraaf, 2015), or will this ultimately save the profession by expanding its jurisdiction (Freidson, 1985; Abbott, 1988)? And in the case of teachers, will the first teachers eventually become deputies, first leaders, or star colleagues (Alvehus et al, 2021)?

I will return to these questions in Chapter 6. (Spoiler alert: It's not a clear-cut process with an easily determined outcome.) What I want to draw attention to here is the agency displayed by professionals in everyday work. To some extent the development of professional elites should be no stranger to a professional. The idea that more senior professionals help their junior colleagues develop in their work, but also monitor their performance and behaviour, should not be alien in professions. The question is, perhaps, not so much of stratification per se, as of how stratification develops. In the ISTC case, even though the professional elite seems to have been rather well integrated in the profession, the elite seemed to orient to a market logic. In the first teacher example, while being an outcome of governmental intervention in the profession and appointed by non-professionals, the first teachers largely seem to have been able to strengthen the profession by internal stratification (Alvehus et al, 2021), but at the same time, some first teachers became more oriented to the bureaucratic logic of school management.

Control over the ambiguity of control

Control is often seen as something imposed – on an organization, or on a work process. The control system itself does not change; it merely changes other things. The common idea that control systems can be 'implemented' manifests this view. The problem is that the view is plain wrong. Control is always a matter of interaction. Control demands the active participation of those controlled. And in professional service organizations, with its highly autonomous work, this issue becomes acute.

In all examples mentioned, from recruitment and career to time and quality control, a recurring theme is how systems of control get subverted. It is difficult to argue that professionals are simply increasingly being subject to control. Instead, control systems cause their own set of ambiguities and problems: how to judge and evaluate performance, how to relate to elite identities, how to make one's way in an up-or-out system.

First, consider the ideal-type professionalism. This involves strong control mechanisms per se. The professional division of labour is one, but there are also reasons for professions and professional service organizations to maintain quality and performance standards within their profession. These come in various guises, from attempts at shaping elite identities to trying to identify performance criteria that are deemed relevant for the profession or professional service organization.

Second, the role of stratification must be acknowledged. Stratification is a profession-relevant way of organizing and is necessary for the profession to maintain in order to take control over the control they are subjected to. The claim to ambiguity is a central component here, as this legitimates the appropriation of control initiatives by elite professionals. The effects of this can vary, and the question of course remains what happens in the long run. Some have argued that it leads to professions becoming increasingly subjected to the external control mechanisms (Bejerot and Hasselbladh, 2011). Yet, again, taking Abbott's (1988) view on professionalism, this would be a natural way for professions to over time adapt to societal expectations and ensuring its own survival by adjusting their jurisdictions – the profession remains but the content of the work changes.

Third, the control forms accounted for do impact the everyday work of professionals. In commercialized client-centred professions, we can expect a strong presence of market logic (Hanlon, 1997), both in terms of the overall goals that the organization pursues, but also in terms of the focus expected from professionals in everyday work (for example, billable hours). It seems quite clear that in professions where up-or-out systems and career concerns dominate, controls have a fairly strong impact on everyday work. Yet also here, the systems are tweaked (game-playing around billable hours and ghosting illustrates this), but the tweaking largely plays into the hands of the objectives of the control systems. Control systems do not get subverted by being gamed; in fact, they seem to intensify workload even more. At the very beginning of this book, I talked about gold-collar proletarians – leverage and up-or-out show that there is some merit to the term.

Thus, as illustrated in this chapter, it is time to drop the idea of professional work being inherently and always autonomous. But we should also drop the idea that it is simply being brought under the control of purportedly objective management and control systems. Things are not as linear and determinate as some observers seem to assume – possibly due to observations made at too high levels of abstraction. (I will return to this problem in Chapter 6.) Professional service organizations are undergoing changes, that much is clear. How these changes actually unfold is a question of empirical investigation and in this we clearly benefit from moving away from a macro perspective, and instead towards understanding institutional logics 'at the coalface' (Barley, 2008).

5

The Politics of Leadership

This chapter takes us into some of the most contested terrain in all of management and organization studies: leadership. On the one hand, we find an almost constant demand for leadership: In society we are said to need leadership in order to manage climate change, poverty, innovation, and all various kinds of problems; in organizations we are said to need relational leadership, coaching leadership, change leadership, authentic transformative leadership – not mere management and administration. And academics produce a seemingly endless stream of studies of the benefits of leadership. Leadership seems to provide a solution to most problems – at least in Western society, we seemingly have a romance with leadership, that is, the term is loaded with positive values, and it is also so vague it can be used to explain almost anything (Meindl et al, 1985; Bligh and Schyns, 2007; Collinson et al, 2018). And on the other hand, when things go wrong, we hear the Queen of Hearts within us demanding the heads of the leaders.

Leadership becomes significant in a professional service context for three reasons. First, the one just mentioned: professional service organizations are no exception to demands for more and better leadership. Quite on the contrary, in fact. As I have shown in the previous chapters, ambiguity plays a key role in professional service work, and ambiguous situations tend to generate calls for clarity – something leadership purportedly provides. Second, leadership in professional service organizations is often of a particular kind: Traditionally, professional service organizations have often had various collective solutions to the 'problem' of leadership, involving shared leadership and different forms of collegial decision-making. Third, leadership in professional service organizations is often referred to as 'herding cats', implying its futility.

In the following, I first highlight common assumptions about leadership in professional service organizations – the idea of 'cat herding'. I will then address the romance of leadership, followed by a discussion on leadership theory. These are necessary in order to set a theoretical stage for the further discussion: how leadership is accomplished in professional service organizations through legitimizing, negotiating, and manoeuvring. Finally I will, once again, come back to the role of ambiguity, this time in leadership processes.

On the herding of cats

You can't really tell people what to do. You can say what you're going to do and then hope people will agree with it … and the people you can least tell what to do are those who are most important for the success of the business. (Empson and Alvehus, 2020, p 1243)

[F]rankly nobody has to follow anyone. (Empson and Alvehus, 2020, p 1243)

The two quotes come from key players in the top leadership echelons of two global, very successful, professional service firms. These firms are certainly no anarchies, yet these managers talk about leadership in ways that almost imply this: 'hope people will agree', 'nobody has to follow'. In this way they express the key professional service organization value of individual autonomy (Empson et al, 2015a). If we look only to this, accomplishing leadership in professional service organizations seems almost impossible.

This idea about how leadership and management happen – or do not happen – in professional service organizations is colloquially referred to as 'herding cats'. The implication is of course that this is an impossible feat. Cats go wherever they want to go, and they do whatever they choose to do. They are not easily herded.[1] Consider, however, this:

Having grown up on a dairy farm, the characterization never made much sense to me. Cows and sheep earn our disparaging remarks because they are easy to push around. Their occasional resistance seems counter to their character. But cats are also easy to herd; just have milk. Cats may walk by themselves, but they quickly all choose to walk in the same direction following the pail. Cats may quickly resist getting pushed in common directions, but they are easily pulled there. Got milk, got cats. (Deetz, 2008, p 387)

---

[1]   In an episode of the television show *Mythbusters* (Discovery Channel), hosts Jamie Hyneman and Adam Savage actually tried to herd cats (Season 12, Episode 6: 'Mythssion Impossible'). They failed spectacularly.

Pull. Don't push. Is it that easy? If so, how is this done? And what is 'milk' in a professional service organization context?

There is no point in getting stuck in the metaphor for too long but one thing to note, and that I will get back to, is the milk issue. It implies that leadership has to do with resources, and thereby with formal structures and the rights and obligations that go with them – but also that other resources, such as knowledge and client contacts, come into play. This means that there is no use trying to establish a clear line between leadership and management, or seeing leadership as disconnected from professional work. Instead, I take the starting point that resources, formal positions, management control, and work processes all play their part in accomplishing leadership. This further means that in the light of this chapter, also the two previous chapters were about the accomplishment of leadership. Here I will however focus more on interpersonal relationships than on the systems per se, but of course this is a largely artificial distinction.

Anyway, what Deetz's dairy farm experience highlights, is that professional service organizations are indeed possible to lead, although they bring out a number of leadership issues that are, if not unique to these organizations, at least easily observed in them.

Two characteristics of professional service organizations that were introduced already in Chapter 2, when I defined the term professional service organization, are important to remember: extensive individual autonomy and contingent managerial authority. Extensive individual autonomy has popped up continuously in this book, and I need not repeat it here; it is a property normally associated with professional work, although it needs to be somewhat qualified (see Chapter 3).

Contingent managerial authority means that a 'leader of professionals may only lead by their consent' and that authority 'is collegial and fragile and deemed to rest with the professional peer group rather than the individual' (Empson, 2017, p 21). In some cases, this is formalized. In professional service organizations it is not uncommon to see different forms of collegiality, and professional service firms are often structured as professional partnerships in terms of ownership. A partnership ownership makes a lot of sense in a situation where the assets are almost exclusively immaterial and bound up in individual knowledge, experience, and client relationships (Greenwood et al, 1990; von Nordenflycht, 2010). It also somewhat emblemizes professional service firms, and many organizations mimic it (Empson and Chapman, 2006). In other cases, collegiality is built into the legislative structure of the organization, as in old-school universities that are still ran by collegiums; arguably a suitable form for running universities (Sahlin and Eriksson-Zetterquist, 2016). In these kinds of formal arrangements, leaders are literally in the hands of the presumed followers: one unsuccessful election, and they have to leave. Non-professional leaders can have a hard time gaining influence, and perhaps find themselves trying to herd cats. Their authority is contingent on the acceptance of the professional workers.

I have, together with Laura Empson, argued that this gives rise to a set of processes that together make the leadership situation in professional service organizations quite fragile: legitimizing, negotiating, and manoeuvring (Empson and Alvehus, 2020). But, before exploring these in detail, I need to expand somewhat on the concept of leadership.

The romance of leadership

Leaders serve as symbols and scapegoats, and by leadership we seem to be able to explain almost anything that is going on in organizations, good or bad. This was noted over 30 years ago, when Meindl et al (1985) argued that we – scholars and society in general – have a 'romance with leadership'. They argued that the term leadership in itself is vague and can encompass almost anything and that, therefore, it serves very well to explain that which we cannot understand. They wrote:

> It appears that as observers of and as participants in organizations, we may have developed highly romanticized, heroic views of leadership – what leaders do, what they are able to accomplish, and the general effects they have on our lives. One of the principal elements in this romanticized conception is the view that leadership is a central organizational process and the premier force in the scheme of organizational events and activities. (Meindl et al, 1985, p 79)

This romance with leadership seems to go on. Despite research continuously showing a lack of evidence when it comes to specific leadership traits, or clear connections between leader style–situation–effectiveness, or the problematic status of concepts such as 'transformational leadership', the interest in these and similar ideas does not seem to wear off.[2] The term leadership itself seems to have taken on an almost Velcro-like character: you can throw anything at it, and it will stick (Alvehus, 2021). Moreover, many seem to want leadership to be something inherently good. Leadership researchers sometimes refer to this as 'the Hitler problem': many leadership enthusiasts do not want to

---

[2]   The critique is extensive. Good starting points are introductory books such as Grint (2010) and Schedlitzki and Edwards (2018). Tourish (2019) provides an elaborate critique of authentic leadership. Regarding transformative leadership, see Alvesson and Einola (2019).

include power abuse and the dark sides of leadership in their leadership talk. That is supposedly something other than leadership 'proper', an anomaly to be explained (away). Similarly, questions of organizational politics – for example manipulation, talking behind others' backs, or the withholding of information – are rarely discussed at the same time as leadership (see, however, Watson, 2001; Ammeter et al, 2002). Yet, anyone who has ever worked in an organization knows that these are quite persistent elements in organizational life. Thus, the romance of leadership is a rather problematic circumstance, in that it also affects the way in which we as participants in everyday organizational life engage with leaders and leadership. Meindl et al concluded:

> One plausible hypothesis is that the development of a romanticized conception of leadership causes participants more readily to imbue the symbolic gestures of leaders with meaning and significance. Accordingly, the psychological readiness to comprehend things in terms of leadership, whatever dysfunctions it represents, may play an important role in determining the ultimate effectiveness of symbolism as a political tool, benefiting most those leaders who are adept at its manipulation. (Meindl et al, 1985, pp 99–100)

The critique against romanticized notions of leadership is extensive, and it has been repeated over the years (Bligh and Schyns, 2007; Collinson et al, 2018). I will leave it for now. What I would like to draw attention to is the very last part of the quotation: 'leaders who are adept at its manipulation'. As has been the case throughout this book, I keep an eye on agency, and this chapter is no exception. There are reasons to look a bit more closely into what people actually do, when they 'do leadership'. But this demands a brief excursion in recent leadership theories, more specifically the notions of *collective* and *distributed* leadership.

Leadership as a collective and distributed phenomenon

Leadership researchers have only recently started to show an interest in understanding leadership as a dynamic, interpersonal process. This should, to an outsider, come as a bit of a surprise. Of course leadership is an interpersonal process! In fact, most definitions emphasize that it is (see Rost, 1993, whose assessment of leadership research is still relevant). And the phenomenon of influence in interpersonal interaction has been explored for many, many years in social and group psychology. Even more, pioneering management writer Mary Parker Follett wrote about this a hundred years ago (a number of her essays are collected in Follett, 2013). To be honest, leadership research is embarrassingly slow to the table. (I see myself as a leadership researcher, so I can say this.)

Anyway, the understanding of leadership as an interactive, dynamic process has become rather popular of late, and has reinvigorated leadership studies by engaging in studying leadership in practice, as it is accomplished in everyday work. Terms such as collective leadership, shared leadership, distributed leadership, co-constructed leadership, and leadership-as-practice, to name a few, abound. Largely, these can be sorted into two main orientations regarding what this collective dimension amounts to, both of which are relevant in this context. (For an overview, see Denis et al, 2012.)

The first is understanding leadership as collective in the sense of a structure for how to handle the problem of leading organizations. We can, for example, talk about dyadic leadership, where two individuals share leader responsibilities, or leadership that is shared by a broader leadership constellation. In professional contexts, such models are not uncommon. Collegial structures, for example, sometimes imply different forms of shared leadership and participative decision-making (Sahlin and Eriksson-Zetterquist, 2016). However, collective leadership structures need not to be formalized, or very democratic either. Sometimes a 'shadow government' rules the organization (Empson, 2017). Often, although not always, these notions of collective leadership carry with them ideals of democracy and they have been accused of harbouring a 'naïve democratic ideal in which leadership is an organizational quality shared by all' (Denis et al, 2012, p 274) and of understating the role of power (Alvehus, 2019b).

A second and completely different understanding of the collective dimension is when it is understood as an inherent element in all leadership processes. In this view, leadership is always an outcome of the interaction between people. Power, influence, and leadership are therefore phenomena that must be understood as distributed in social systems – they do not reside 'in' or 'with' individuals. In this process all participants have agency, although agency is always circumscribed by the situation in different ways. This is well illustrated by Latour's power paradox: 'when you simply *have* power – *in potentia* – nothing happens and you are powerless; when you *exert* power – *in actu* – *others* are performing the action and not you' (Latour, 1986, pp 264–265). Any social activity depends on the actions of those involved, no matter who turns out to be leader and who turns out to be follower; such role assignments are by themselves an outcome of interaction, not a cause of it (DeRue and Ashford, 2010). Leadership is, in this view, a distributed process of accomplishing direction (Crevani, 2018; Alvehus and Crevani, forthcoming). In the leadership process, various kinds of activities are included, even those shied away from in romanticized accounts of leadership – including politics and manipulation – and this therefore invites a view on leadership that also includes the 'dirty' elements in the process (Alvehus, 2021). It also means that the distinction between leadership and management becomes blurry and often quite pointless. Management, formal structures, and control over resources will influence the leadership process as they are contextual elements that cannot be ignored.

We must be careful to keep these two different notions of the collective dimension in leadership apart. The first is a model or structure, a way of arranging situations for enabling certain forms of leadership; the second is a question of ontology. For the purposes of this book, I will use the term *collective leadership* as a label for arrangements where leadership is deliberately shared, formally or informally, among several people (the first understanding). The general view I have on leadership is that it is a *distributed* phenomenon (the second understanding), and therefore I see leadership as an outcome of social processes. I can't really draw unequivocally on established terminology here. At the time of writing the terminology is a bit confused in the leadership research community. It might turn out that when the terminology stabilizes, other terms are used, or my stipulative definitions here have changed places. (I guess at that point I will get a reason to make a second edition of this book.)

The perspective I take on leadership enables asking the question: Which social processes are involved in accomplishing leadership? This means that when discussing leadership, I will draw attention to structural arrangements and formal positions, as these are undeniably relevant as they influence the distributed leadership process, albeit we cannot reduce discussions of leadership to only about these. Quite the contrary. We certainly need to address the way in which different actors act, in order to understand how leadership is accomplished – leadership is about interactions and how roles such as 'leader' and 'follower' are negotiated in interaction (DeRue and Ashford, 2010; Empson and Alvehus, 2020). And it makes sense to think that different people have different skill sets in this regard, and that these come into play in different ways in different situations.

With this in mind, we can get to the meat of this chapter: How is leadership in professional service organizations accomplished?

Legitimizing: role modelling to lead

The words 'leader' and 'leadership' have, Schedlitzki and Edwards (2018, p 16) claim, their origin in the Anglo-Saxon word 'laeder', meaning 'a road' or 'a path'. A path is something that gives direction and it is something you can choose to follow, literally and metaphorically, and in this imagery lies one key aspect to leadership in professional contexts.

For a person in a managerial position in a professional service organization to gain followers, it is key to have professional legitimacy – to be recognized by one's peers as a person who has a profound understanding of the job. Professionals, as expressed by a respondent, 'will accept almost unlimited decision making and authority from someone that they think understands the things they are going through' (Empson, 2017, p 45). There is basically a strong element of trust tied to being seen as able to deliver. In a study of health care medical managers, one manager argued:

> if I devoted more time to it [managerial tasks] and, say, only did five sessions – I know someone who is half and half like that – I would lose the confidence of my colleagues. They would say 'He's no longer a proper doctor'. For my professional well-being I want to be full-time, you've got to see a healthy number of patients to keep up your skills, you can become de-skilled very quickly. (Llewellyn, 2001, pp 604–605)

Professional performance is a rather vague criterion, which stems from the ambiguity of professional work and the difficulty of establishing relevant performance metrics. In the firms studied in Empson and Alvehus (2020), the relevant performance metric was success in the market: bringing in clients, making deals, and expanding the business were important to be seen as successful; what is sometimes referred to as being a 'rainmaker'. In the case of medicine from Llewellyn (2001), it was about keeping up the time spent with patients. Another example is in today's academia, where it is increasingly important to publish in top-tier academic journals (instead of, for example, writing books). While not a universally or unequivocally accepted criterion (see, for example, Alvesson et al, 2017, for a critique) it has increasingly become a performance metric to be reckoned with.

For an individual to reach top positions in the professional service organizations studied by Empson (2017) and Empson and Alvehus (2020), professional legitimacy was a *sine qua non* – without it, nothing. But, as Empson and Alvehus note, we need to be a bit more detailed about what comprises this professional legitimacy. It must be recognized as an interpersonal process, a dynamic between someone performing and some others inferring leadership ability from this. Different professions and different organizations will have different such ways of displaying success and continued performance within the professional work. In a study of physicians, Andersson (2015) emphasized the role of maintaining a medical identity as a strategically important choice for managers. One medical manager said:

> I think I provoked people more during the first years I was manager. I thought I had 'seen the light' through improvement science

and I wanted to implement my ideas, I directed people too much. Especially my physician colleagues reacted in a sour manner. Several times I heard 'I don't have time for this crap, I need to take care of my patients'. Now I have taken a few steps back and talk to my physician colleagues as colleagues. I think I have re-gained some of my influence, a strategy of 'help it happen' has worked better than one of 'make it happen'. (Andersson, 2015, p 92)

Here, we see the legitimacy played out in terms of the strategic use of identity. The process of legitimizing takes place in interpersonal relationships.

The legitimizing process may at first glance appear rather one-sided: A person performs in a way that others perceive as good, and these persons then attribute leadership qualities. But, if we look to the importance of the master–apprentice relationship in the professional division of labour, the role of superior knowledge in creating leadership legitimacy makes sense. It is embedded in the way in which professional work is organized. When discussing the mentor–protégé relationship in large accounting firms, Dirsmith et al (1997) show how relationships could span 'decades and even generations of mentor-protégé dyads' (p 14). In these relationships, the protégé benefited from getting insight into the internal politics of the organization, and in terms of how to relate to formal control systems. But there was a clear reciprocity in the relationships; for example, the mentors gained political influence that extended further in the relationship network. Thus, the master–apprentice structure mirrored in the mentoring relationships might also play a role in the legitimizing process.

But individual professional proficiency is no guarantee for organizational success. Sennett (2008) tells the story of Antonio Stradivari, an excellent craftsman creating masterpieces that are still, 300 years after their making, held in the highest regard. Yet, he failed to pass on his excellence to his two sons, and the secrets of his violin-making died with him. Sennett argues that 'in a workshop where the master's individuality and distinctiveness dominate, tacit knowledge is also likely to dominate. Once the master dies, all the clues, moves, and insights he or she has gathered into the totality of the work cannot be reconstructed' (Sennett, 2008, p 78). Being an excellent craftsperson – or professional – is not enough.

Division of labour is key to the organization of professional work. In this, arguably, lies an element of leadership. The insight from Dirsmith et al (1997) illustrates that this is also related to the politics of the organization, which is something I will return to later. What the failure of the Stradivari workshop tells us, is that this leadership element is crucial in everyday work. A proficient professional worker needs, for the long-term benefit of the organization, to allow the apprentices to expand their professional undertaking from the initial peripheral positions, to full participation. Role modelling is key in this, and this demands participation in the professional division of labour. Yet, this is not always so straightforward. For one thing, scale of operations sometimes invites a more exploitative relationship between different professionals – up-or-out systems come to mind (see Chapter 4). The image of a well-functioning professional workshop becomes, in the light of that, somewhat rose-tinted. Moreover, there is a point in the ambiguity embedded in the division of labour, in that it fosters the kind of autonomy held in such high regard in many professions (see Chapter 3).

The normative lesson here is that leadership cannot be reduced to professional role modelling. Just because someone is good at their work – in terms of billing clients or meeting patients – does not mean that they are a good person or that they have genuine motives. But at the same time, a thorough understanding of the profession's work seems significant not only for professionals striving for top positions, but also for professional service organization performance.

Legitimacy and organizational performance

Sometimes it is argued that who is in charge of organizations matters little, and in many cases this is a reasonable assumption. Top managers have limited influence on the everyday work of most people in a large organization, and, for example, corporate performance depends on conditions outside the control of managers (financial markets, competitors' moves, development of the economy in general). Put bluntly, luck outweighs skill when it comes to the performance of top executives (Piketty, 2014). In many cases the power ascribed to top managers is highly exaggerated – likely an effect of the romance of leadership. However, at least in professional service organizations there are indications that a top leader having a good understanding of how the organization's core 'business' works has some distinct advantages.

In a study of the performance of research universities, Amanda Goodall (2009) shows a causality between the academic performance of the top leaders and the performance of the university. In short, universities where top researchers take top leadership positions start to perform better. The need for specific 'management skills' seems limited. Goodall's explanation for this is fourfold. First, they have credibility – just as the studies mentioned earlier argue. Second, the expert knowledge of the core business – research – provides a 'deep understanding' (2009, p 99) of what the work at university is about, and what conditions need to be in place for successful work to happen. Third, they function as 'standard bearers', in that they have themselves achieved a high level of performance, and therefore their expectation of similar performance from others becomes more legitimate – they may become legitimate role models. This again shows the connection between leadership and how formal control systems work in practice. Fourth, just as top managers in general, they are taken as symbols for what the organization stands for. This also has practical effects, such as increased ability to attract funding.

Interestingly, Goodall also draws parallels to other areas, and specifically US basketball. There, too, she shows, performance of teams is related to previous performance of coaches. Coaches who were themselves good players, become more successful in coaching.

The rather trivial observation that people who are good at what they are doing are more likely to be able to make others good at the same thing, is sobering. The failure throughout the history of leadership studies to find specific leadership skills or traits may primarily be due to leadership researchers' dream of finding something uniquely 'leadery' that can legitimize their area of study. But leadership researchers may have been barking up the wrong tree. Perhaps the key to leading is not something specifically 'leadery', but mainly the ability to be good at the job itself – at least it seems to play an important part in professional service organizations.

Negotiating: managing the 'what's in it for me?' factor

Formal organizations are, among other things, systems for distributing resources, and managers are in the positional power to make decisions over such resources. This means that resources need to be negotiated. Moreover, and as noted in Chapter 4, professional service organizations just like any other formal organization have their fair share of control systems, and these systems are of course most of the time operated by people. A partner in a large professional service organization in Empson and Alvehus (2020) says:

> Partners say 'you're too tight' and they say 'get looser'. So you get looser and they say 'it's chaotic, get tighter'. If the money is going up, you can do what you like. If the money is going down, you can't do anything. But the money going up or down isn't within control of the senior partner. (Empson and Alvehus, 2020, p 1244)

There are demands for control activities. It's easy to guess that such activities are often directed towards 'others, not me'. But if a manager tightens up too much, this might get her into trouble and make her lose the trust of her peers. At the same time, too loose controls are problematic, too. There need to be ways of reining in those who go astray. Moreover, there might be cases where for example different professionals compete for the same clients, things that need to be resolved in one way or another.

Just like legitimizing, negotiating is a dynamic process. Professionals want to feel that they have a high degree of autonomy that they can exercise, yet at the same time there is a need for at least some control over them. Managers in professional service organizations constantly need to balance between these two. This of course becomes particularly salient in organizations where governance is partnership based or in other forms of collegiality, where the manager's future is directly in the hand of her peers.

Put in slightly jaunty terms, the 'WIIFM' factor – *what's in it for me?* – seems to play a significant part in professional service organizations. Leadership is enacted in relationships between professionals, and at the top of the organization between professional peers. Their expectation of autonomy makes leadership 'a matter of guiding, nudging, and persuading' (Greenwood et al, 1990, p 748) – pulling the cats with milk. The expectation of autonomy is often backed up by individual professionals controlling key resources, such as client relationships. 'The one who owns the client relation is king in his own country' as a respondent in Alvehus (2017, p 419) put it.

Again, we see how leadership and the potential for influence cannot be disconnected from organizational context. On the one hand, the way in which hierarchies are tied to resources, and a perceived need for ensuring that other professionals are kept under some sort of observation, mean that there is an expectation on individuals in formal leadership positions to assert some degree of control in the organization. On the other hand, expectations of autonomy paired with actual control over key resources (knowledge, client relationships) mean that control is in a constant balance with the exercising of autonomy. This, in turn, should draw our attention to the role of political astuteness.

Manoeuvring: the importance of seeming earnest

Organizational politics is a term often frowned upon. Yet, for anyone who has been part of an organization, it will be a familiar theme. How to prepare for decision-making by framing information, how some are left out of a decision process, alliances upwards, disassociation from failure, and so on. But are organizational politics only a question of 'reprehensible images that include ... backroom manipulation, behind-the-scenes maneuvering, and self-serving posturing' (Ammeter et al, 2002, p 753)?

The argument put forth by a few scholars, such as the just mentioned Ammeter et al (2002), is that it is not. Organizational politics, in this view, is a naturally occurring element in organizations, and is basically the question of how things get done. It is a necessary practice in organizations (Pfeffer, 1981) and we should perhaps ask ourselves, before throwing the concept of politics out, what an organization *without* politics would be like? A place with no room for influence and no distribution of power whatsoever?

The negative image of organizational politics is also expressed by practitioners. Overt political behaviour is abhorred by the professionals in Empson and Alvehus (2020):

> To me politics smacks of alliance building in the corridors, in offices behind the scenes. It smacks of people engineering agendas, which creep up on the firm and deliver fait accompli or behave in ways that become disruptive. Or politics could manifest as someone undermining another person. I would like to think we don't have those behaviours in this firm. (Empson and Alvehus, 2020, p 1245)

There are strong negative connotations with regards to politics, yet the firms studied were organized as partnerships. This meant that there were elections to top leadership positions and there were clear political activities in terms of election campaigns, rallying speeches, and such. People in leadership positions talked about their 'constituents' and the 'mandate' given to them (Empson and Alvehus, 2020, p 1245). Thus, politics were recognized on one level but at the same time refuted.

On a practical level, political behaviour was clearly manifest. One common element was the need for creating coalitions and support for decisions:

> If there's an idea, a sort of major initiative, it will start with the inner circle. Then it will get the air cover from the board ... As it develops and it's got some legs [the senior partner] will involve one or two other heads of offices ... and there will just be a sort of few people here and there. Then, if the thing is going to happen, there will be a call of all the heads of major offices and all the heads of the other practice groups to get their views before launching it on the partnership. (Empson and Alvehus, 2020, p 1245)

The process described by this partner is one of incrementally building support for an initiative, spreading virally throughout the organization before seeking more formal support. This also means that it is of key significance to know one's networks and where informal power resides, what Empson (2017, p 35) refers to as the 'key influencers', people that 'may have no formal leadership role but have considerable informal power, derived from their client relationships, valuable technical knowledge, and strong reputations'. Despite the verbalized abhorrence of political behaviour there is a clear recognition of the need for such behaviour, although it is framed in less political language.

Given the negative view of politics, it is perhaps not surprising that being caught with trying to 'do politics' is in itself something problematic. In order to be eligible for higher positions, and in order to earn the trust of one's peers, it is important to appear sincere. The Empson and Alvehus (2020) study highlights how leaders should avoid being seen as 'a player' and instead appear as if their motives are authentic and that they are always operating in the best interests of the firm, that '[the firm] is stamped on their heart if you open them up' (p 1246).

> Sometimes my sense would be [senior partner] doesn't necessarily always understand how influential he is. He's very modest about it, quite self-effacing, and he himself doesn't attach such great importance to some of those things that might be under the heading of creeping as in slightly sinister. He is not himself a player in that way at all ... it's simply because his own motivations in this world are so, I think, very genuine and clean. (Empson and Alvehus, 2020, p 1245)

It is of course naïve to assume that someone aiming for the top of a global and highly successful firm, with fierce competition for leadership positions, would do this without any self-interest. Yet interestingly, this is the view that these professionals hold of their elected leaders. It seems displaying a reluctance to take on the leader role is quite favourable (Andersson, 2005) – there is an importance of seeming earnest.

Underneath the polished surface there is a political undergrowth in the organization that we need to understand, if we want to understand how leader–follower relationships are accomplished. The firms studied by Empson (2017) and Empson and Alvehus (2020) are extreme cases of peer-to-peer relationships. They may thus not be representative in a statistical sense, but they do highlight processes that are otherwise less easy to observe. Because, also in contexts where professionalism is not only about peers, but about superordinate–subordinate relationships, the role of political manoeuvring comes through. Kellogg (2019) studied how two hospitals tried to implement patient-centred medical home reforms, and in a comparative analysis shows that recruiting subordinate semi-professionals can be a valuable way of influencing professionals. In the reform, it turned out that recruiting the low-status medical assistants was a key to success:

> subordinate semi-professionals, despite having no formal authority over professionals, have a high capacity for influence derived from their favorable structural position. When they occupy a central position in the professionals' workflow, they can control professionals' access to information about new practices and can offer professionals opportunities

for consultation about these practices before implementation. When they perform tasks that are critical to professionals' daily work, they can ask for favors of them. When they occupy a central position in the professionals' peer network, they can convert one or two professionals and then tell the others about the new practices peers are using. And when they are positioned between the client and the professional, they can suggest changes in professional practice while also shielding professionals from the emotional challenges of upset or angry clients. (Kellogg, 2019, p 957)

The example shows that in complex professional service organizations, we cannot look at single professionals or single professions. Politics is about understanding an organization as a political ecosystem, where all parts are to some extent interlocked in the flow of everyday work. And it is impossible to sidestep the role of formal authority relations and control over resources in discussing leadership – as Kellogg's example clearly illustrates, we need to understand leadership processes as distributed and depending on interaction; those presumably influenced actively influence how they become influenced. And, this interaction and political processes are embedded in everyday work.

Leadership as an unstable equilibrium

All the three relational processes identified – legitimizing, negotiating, and manoeuvring – should be understood as just that: processes, taking place over time. Together, they constitute an instable equilibrium: 'leadership dynamics are in perpetual flux, moving through periods of destabilization and stabilization, but never achieving a stable equilibrium' (Empson and Alvehus, 2020, p 1247). This is, again, something that is also the case in any organization, but in a context of extensive individual autonomy and contingent managerial authority (Empson et al, 2015a) they become accentuated. Destabilization may be triggered by imbalances in any of the three relational processes.

First, declining success in the marketplace may cause professionals to infer that a colleague no longer has the ability to lead them. Second, asserting too much control may cause professionals to infer that a colleague is preventing them from exercising their autonomy, and asserting too little control may cause professionals to judge them as ineffective. Third, being seen to act politically may cause professionals to infer that a colleague lacks integrity. (Empson and Alvehus, 2020, p 1250)

Leadership is a distributed phenomenon, and the accomplishment of leadership cannot be disassociated from formal and informal structures of authority, and it cannot be understood without considering the way in which it relates to professional work. Moreover, the leadership dynamics in turn affect the formal and informal power relationships in the organization. Some professional service organizations, in this chapter mainly exemplified by professional partnerships, adopt collective leadership structures, where these processes become clearly distinguishable.

The hybrid professional–manager

In general, as professions have increasingly become tied to and dependent upon large formal organizations, management has also become professionalized. As should be clear from this chapter, viewing leadership and management as separate from the 'core' professional work is problematic. On the other hand, many contexts are multiprofessional, and of course the question of which profession can and should take on managerial responsibilities arises. Moreover, as noted in Chapter 4, stratification is a way of protecting professional jurisdictions. This has led to the rise of hybrid professional–manager roles that blur the distinctions between professional and bureaucratic logic (Kirkpatrick, 2016). Llewellyn (2001) has described these roles as 'two-way windows', where (in her case) clinical directors occupy positions where they mediate between professional and bureaucratic logics. Professionals seem to be 'more advantageously positioned than managers to occupy the "two-way" space opened up by mediation; managerial work being more permeable, and therefore, more easily appropriated, than professional work' (Llewellyn, 2001, p 618). Just as in Kellogg's (2019) study, intermediate positions controlling resources and flow of information seem particularly efficient in affecting the direction of the organization. But the process identified by Llewellyn also allows managerial discourses to enter the professional vocabulary and thereby possibly operating as a Trojan horse, sneaking its way into professionalism and eventually overpowering it: 'The established professional regime, until recently uncontested in its authority over medical practice, is silently dying', as Bejerot and Hasselbladh (2011, p 1618) dramatically put it in a study of quality registers in health care.

The outcome of these processes, and the struggle for power over everyday professional work, is not easily determined. In Chapter 6 I will return to the question of hybridity, and to how we can conceptualize these power struggles.

The romantic ambiguity of leadership

In the assumption that leadership is of key importance, it is often the more romantic view of leadership that comes into play. Leaders should inspire, provide vision, and transform organizations. Certain leader qualities are sought after. Leadership in this sense is, however, arguably of little significance in general, and in professional service organizations in particular. On the other hand, cat herding seems an inapt analogy. Leadership in professional service organizations is more complex than either romance or cat herding implies. Understanding leadership as a distributed process opens up for a very different, and less romantic, view of leadership.

First, let me return to a note I made in the beginning of the chapter, regarding leadership and management. Insofar as leadership is understood as a distributed phenomenon, a sharp distinction between leadership and management – a classic suggestion of this is Zaleznik (1977) – becomes rather pointless. As I have shown, management control technologies, resource allocation, and formal authority is all part of the negotiation process and thus part of accomplishing leadership.

Leadership, in the broader sense in which I approach it here, indeed seems to be of some importance in professional service organizations. Arguably, leadership is accomplished in a complex process of legitimizing, negotiating, and manoeuvring. For leaders to gain the legitimacy to lead, professional skills are significant. But these skills also seem to play a part in the efficient operation of professional service organizations. They provide a thorough understanding of the ambiguities of professional work that is key for leading them. And, arguably, professionals apt at negotiating and skilful political manoeuvring will likely have an advantage in getting to leadership positions. But seeing these aspects depends on a distributed and empirically sensitive understanding of leadership, as they are not generally associated with leadership: legitimizing is about professional work, not leadership; negotiating over resources is more commonly associated with management, not leadership; and political manoeuvring is often not associated with leadership at all. Thus, the discussion in this chapter opens up for a new view of what skills might be important in leadership. But those skills are not the romanticized leadership skills; rather they are about performing in everyday work, about formal hierarchies, and about navigating and manipulating interpersonal relationships in a complex political milieu.

Some professional service organizations adopt leadership structures of collective character. From the characteristics of professional work, this makes sense. It is difficult to see the relevance of more grandiose ideas about leadership (such as transformative leadership) in these contexts. Yet, these organizations of course also have their heroes and role models. 'War stories' of difficult client contracts, last-minute efforts of finishing projects, and dramatic solutions to urgent problems of course abound. But in the light of this chapter, it is hard to see this as qualifying for the label leadership. Instead, we should understand these stories and anecdotes as part of the imagery of leadership, providing legitimacy and evidence of professional competence and personal integrity, so key for legitimizing and manoeuvring. In this sense, romantic images of leadership become part of even more romanticized views on leadership. The romance of leadership reproduces itself not only by making recipients of leadership ready to 'imbue the symbolic gestures of leaders with meaning and significance' (Meindl et al, 1985, p 100), but also by denying the 'dirty' everyday leadership work that underlies it (Alvehus, 2021).

This chapter thus brings in another dimension to the discussion of ambiguity. On the one hand, we find managing – or at least appearing to manage – profession-relevant ambiguity important in gaining legitimacy. But to this comes the ambiguity always involved in political processes, where the motives of others, and the motives one attributes to others, become significant. Appearing genuine and clean is one thing – and what personal aspirations lurk behind the façade, another. Ambiguity has a function in that it blurs this incongruity.

6

Superficial Hybridity

Recently, the notion of the 'hybrid organization' has become rather popular, especially in the context of professional service organizations. It is hard to trace the origins of the term, and its meaning is somewhat unclear – in the context of discussions of professions, the earliest use I have been able to trace was Wilensky (1964). Whatever hybrid means in this context it is however hard to argue that it is something fundamentally new, despite often being marketed as such – the standard 'everything is changing so fast and becoming so complex that organizations have to find new solutions'-rhetoric. The newness probably lies in the term rather than the phenomenon, as is all too often the case in the social sciences. Judging from the literature on professional service organizations in the last few years, these organizations have seemingly undergone a tremendous shift in the way they are managed, governed, and structured. Previously, it is said, they were dominated by a professional logic. Increasingly, however, this logic has been challenged by bureaucratic logic or market logic (or other logics), and this has given rise to new, hybrid organizational forms. Professionals in such hybrids are in one way or another forced to deal with several, possibly inconsistent or conflicting, institutional logics in their everyday work.

I will, at the end of this chapter, return to whether this view has merit – I am generally sceptical. But first, we need to look into what this whole notion of hybridity means, and how it has been dealt with in theorizing. After this I discuss three dominant hypotheses on how hybridity plays out in organizations: the degradation hypothesis, the harmony hypothesis, and the loose couplings hypothesis. After this I start problematizing the notion of hybridity more fundamentally, explicitly drawing on the way I theorized institutional logics in Chapter 2. I then continue by suggesting a fourth hypothesis with which to understand hybridity: superficial hybridity, and I finish the chapter by suggesting that conflicts between institutional logics should primarily be understood in terms of redundancy.

What is hybridity?

Hybrid organizations, broadly speaking, are organizations that encompass several, potentially conflicting, institutional logics and blend these. This leads to the assumption that such organizations have to deal with a certain, and unique, set of organizational problems, that do not appear in 'pure' organizational forms. This use of the term 'hybrid' is in line with dictionary definitions. According to the Merriam-Webster dictionary, a hybrid is 'an offspring of two animals or plants of different races ... breeds, varieties, species, or genera'. More generally it is defined as 'something heterogeneous in origin or composition'. Often, such hybridity is sought for in institutional environments where the several logics coexist (Reay and Hinings, 2009; Alvehus and Andersson, 2018). Common examples are organizations with both profit and not-for-profit concerns or, as in the theme of this book, organizations where professional logics coincide with market logic and/or bureaucratic logic. However, we need to be observant on whether the term hybrid refers to organizations operating in environments with conflicting institutional logics, on the one hand, and hybrid organizational forms, on the other. It is, at least theoretically, possible to imagine single-logic organizations in a hybrid environment, or hybrid organizations in a single-logic environment. In this chapter, in line with the ambitions of this book, I am primarily concerned with hybrid organizational forms – the focus is on work and management in organizations.

Another issue is so-called constitutional hybrids (Alexius and Furusten, 2019), organizations that by design involve different stakeholders, such as a for-profit firm owned by a municipality. In such organizations goal-conflict will likely be salient. But calling any incongruency in goals in the organization 'hybridity' might stretch the concept of hybridity too far – few organizations are free from goal conflicts. Again, I will here primarily discuss hybridity in terms of ideal-typical institutional logics, and such may of course become manifest in, for example, formal structures or ownership arrangements, but need not be.

The literature on hybridity seldom restricts the notion of institutional logics to the three ideal types in Freidson (2001). Instead, many different labels of logics appear, often identified in a particular context and with unspecified relations to more overarching notions of institutional logics, value spheres, or institutional orders – which incidentally is a bit odd, since the whole point of the term 'institutional logics', when it was popularized by Friedland and Alford (1991), was to 'bring society back in'. In general, the use of the term 'logic' is rather vague. This is in itself not necessarily a problem, but the reader should be aware that there are somewhat different conceptualizations that influence also the accounts here.

Another meaning of the term hybrid, again from Merriam-Webster, is 'something (such as a power plant, vehicle, or electronic circuit) that has two different types of components performing essentially the same function'. Hybridity here implies redundancy, an overlap of different functions. I will return to this; it is an aspect of hybridity seldom explored, but I think it is key for understanding what hybridity, to the extent that this term is at all necessary, really is about in organizational contexts. But before I get there, I need to explore the way in which hybridity is discussed in the professional service organization context today.

An example from the world of finance will illustrate: Battilana and Dorado's (2010) study of micro-finance in Bolivia. Two non-governmental organizations (NGOs) providing micro loans found the demand so large, they decided to launch commercial organizations in order to meet it: BancoSol and Los Andes saw the light of day. This made the NGOs subject to not only the development logic of the not-for-profit endeavour of improving life for the poor, but also to the logic of financial markets and regulations. Thus, they found themselves operating in the intersection of different logics that put conflicting demands on the organizations: 'The development logic pressed them to retain their mission of providing access to financial services to those excluded from the conventional financial sector, while the banking logic simultaneously pressed them to fulfil the fiduciary obligations of commercial financial institutions' (Battilana and Dorado, 2010, p 1423). So, a previously idealistic not-for-profit organization has suddenly become also a commercial financial institution. This situation meant that the organizations had to deal with conflicting sets of demands, and Battilana and Dorado note that such a feat is often difficult to pull off and maintain in the long run. The organizations in this case tried to develop new identities by for example socialization; as one of the respondents in the study memorably put it, by 'converting social workers into bankers and bankers into social workers' (Battilana and Dorado, 2010, p 1426). In one organization, BancoSol, this was not very successful. Eventually the conflict assumed such proportions that the 'social worker' category was almost eradicated from BancoSol.

The other organization, Los Andes, was more successful. The socialization strategy was markedly different, for example focusing more on 'hard' performance measures than intersubjective judgement and they maintained a focus on 'operational excellence' (Battilana and Dorado, 2010, p 1430). Systems for hiring, selection, and performance measurement were more transparent and fostered meritocracy. 'Creating a shared identity based on operational excellence seems to have enabled Los Andes to strike a sustainable balance between the development and banking logics and to avoid mission drift' (Battilana and Dorado, 2010, p 1431). The new identity enabled the employees to 'strike a balance' between the logics of development and banking in one case; in the other case, the outcome was the dominance of one logic. Hybrids thus find it difficult to achieve this balance between logics, and we would expect stability in hybridity to be a fragile affair. If it fails, one logic will succumb to the other.

Views on how hybridity becomes manifest in organizations, and its consequences, vary. If we look at the literature on hybridity and professionalism, there are broadly speaking three hypotheses that compete for attention. First, there is the *degradation hypothesis*, stating that professional logics will eventually succumb to the logics of the market and the bureaucracy. Second, the *harmony hypothesis*. This is quite the opposite, and states that organizations can sustain competing and conflicting institutional logics at the same time by integrating them. Third, the *loose coupling hypothesis* similarly to the harmony hypothesis states that organizations sustain multiple logics, not by integrating them but by separating them from each other; there is still tension, but it is managed.

The degradation hypothesis

The degradation hypothesis understands professional work as ideally, and historically, dominated by professional logic. When a professional logic meets with other logics, most often that of the market or that of bureaucracy, the professional logic eventually loses the battle. Professional work becomes deprived of its unique qualities – autonomy, independent application of abstract knowledge, freedom to develop client relations, and so on. It becomes degraded, subject to external controls and accountability, and loses its inherent meaningfulness. The extreme view of this can be found already in the 1970s, in Oppenheimer's notion of the proletarianization of the professional: 'a white collar proletarian type of worker is now replacing the autonomous professional type of worker in the upper strata of professional-technical employment' (Oppenheimer, 1972, p 213). Here, we find the pure professional work being supplanted by a proletarian form of work, which Oppenheimer goes on to characterize as:

(a) extensive division of labour exists so that the typical worker performs only one, or a small number, of tasks in a total process; (b) the pace of work, the characteristics of the workplace, the nature of the product, the uses to which it is put, and its market conditions are determined not by the worker, but by higher authorities (private or public bureaucracies); (c) the worker's primary source of income is his wage, which is determined by large-scale market conditions and economic processes (not excluding collective bargaining), rather than by individual face-to-face bargaining; and (d) the worker, in order to defend his situation from deteriorating living and/or working standards, moves toward collective bargaining in some form. (Oppenheimer, 1972, p 213)

Thus, a complete opposite of the ideal-type professional work takes command – compare with the Oppenheimer quote in Chapter 3! Oppenheimer argued that there was a trend towards such proletarianization. Professions are, he argued, increasingly subjected to bureaucratic working conditions and will as a consequence of this become proletarianized. The process is one-directional and deterministic.

Now, Oppenheimer wrote this half a century ago, but we still often find the same line of reasoning represented. The basic idea is that professionalism is a weaker logic, and that other logics – bureaucracy, market, corporate – take over and dominate or even obliterate the professional logic. For example, in discussions about New Public Management (Hood, 1991) it is commonly argued that bureaucratic control forms have come to dominate professional work. The very idea of New Public Management was the last word: management. Importing ideas of free market competition and forms of management from the private sector was thought to be a way of making the inefficient public organizations more reminiscent of private, market-oriented organizations – and thereby making them more efficient. However, 50 years after Oppenheimer we are not even close to this complete degradation of professional work. And, as noted by Evetts (2003), the image of declining professionalism appears simultaneously with the argument that professionalism in society increases and that we more and more rely on experts, in organizational decision-making as well as in everyday life. These two images are difficult to reconcile. One answer is that professions are not homogeneous entities. Within a profession there is a stratification (see Chapter 4) and thus, all professionals do not engage in the same kind of work. For example, in the medical profession, elite professionals have emerged, that buffer the rank-and-file professionals from administrative work and bureaucratic intervention.

A more nuanced take on this demise of professionalism is studies inspired by concepts such as governmentality (drawing on the works of Michel Foucault, for example Foucault, 2008, but see also Rose, 1999). Here, the focus is less on overt domination over professionalism and more on a slow and subtle colonization of professional values. For example, Bejerot and Hasselbladh (2011) argue that physicians are increasingly getting involved in administrative imperatives to manage medical work – their case concerns quality registers in Swedish health care – but in doing this, they start to incorporate these bureaucratic values into their own professionalism, and professionalism is therefore slowly eroded from within. Studying similar cases (including quality registers in Swedish health care), Levay and Waks (2009) however highlight how medical professionals develop 'soft autonomy', a kind of 'professional autonomy which is mitigated by continuous external monitoring but still leaves considerable freedom for professionals to decide on assessment criteria and procedures' (p 523). Similarly, Kirkpatrick and Noordegraaf (2015) argue that professionals increasingly seek legitimacy by appropriating elements of, for example, bureaucratic logic (and thus provide a harmony-inspired counter-argument to the degradation hypothesis; to be discussed in the next section). The question is, of course, whether what we observe is a shift of jurisdictions and opportunistic stratification by professionals, or a determinate process where the logic of professionalism is eventually diminished?

It is hard to shrug off a feeling of romanticism when reading degradation accounts. Professional work, it seems, is all joy and fun whereas work in bureaucracy is all bad: degrading, demeaning, demonized. Such a romanticized image however denies the harsh reality of junior professionals in up-or-out systems, where competition for higher positions leads to interpersonal conflict and, for many, exit. It excludes the development of elite identities and corresponding problems with overwork and careerism. It also excludes the ambiguity of knowledge work and the way in which this is reproduced by structural conditions, enabling exploitation. From a societal point of view it denies the criticism that professions become too powerful and mainly serve their own self-interest (Larson, 1977). And so on. As usual, romanticism is best left out when it comes to understanding the reality of work and organizations.

The harmony hypothesis

A significantly more optimistic view on the potential of professionalism coexisting with other logics is provided by Henry Mintzberg. In his classic book *Structure in Fives*, he argued that the professional bureaucracy provides the professional with 'the best of both worlds: he is attached to an organization, yet is free to serve his client in his own way, constrained only by the established standards of his profession' (Mintzberg, 1983, p 205). This is the harmony hypothesis. The key idea is that professionalism, and professional work processes, can thrive under bureaucratic rule. Now, there is of course a key difference between what Mintzberg meant by bureaucracy, and the way in which bureaucracy is understood from the degradation hypothesis. In Mintzberg's view, bureaucracy seems to regard the context for work; the infrastructure if you like. He argues that professionals are generally not very interested in administration – and really, except for administrators, who is? – and therefore develop support structures that can deal with this. They hire support staff such as clerks and IT personnel to deal with everyday chores, and can thereby focus on the professional work themselves. It is key here to understand Mintzberg's terminology (see Chapter 2). When bureaucracy interferes in the work process it is not a question of administration in Mintzberg's vocabulary: then, it is called technostructure. A professional organization accepts and promotes one aspect of bureaucracy (support staff) but tries to avoid the other (technostructure).

We find a similar view in more recent accounts for the development towards hybridization. Kodeih and Greenwood (2014, p 31), for example, in a study of French business schools, argue that different institutional logics, in their case embodied in identities, can indeed be incorporated and reconciled without 'severing their initial identities'. Alternative logics can in fact become key in seeking out new 'aspirational' identities. Thus, they argue that 'logics per se are not intrinsically incompatible' but that they are constructed as such by actors. A similar argument is made by Kirkpatrick and Noordegraaf. In the literature, they argue, there is often an underlying assumption of a 'pure' form of professional work, embodied by the sole practitioner and contrasted against salaried workers. But 'these assumptions about the mutual exclusivity of professions and organizations have always been open to question and have increasingly become more so' (Kirkpatrick and Noordegraaf, 2015, p 92). Instead, they suggest that we must see that professionals on the one hand have, at least for a long time, in fact been working within the confines of larger bureaucratic structures – prime examples would be physicians in hospitals or accountants in large accounting firms. As I have pointed out, they also note that this is sometimes an attractive solution, sought out by professionals. The challenges facing professionals today, including increased demand for accountability, a strife for increased or at least maintained legitimacy, and changing demographics (predominantly, an increased femininization of professionalism) all make more bureaucratic forms of organizing a viable and attractive option for professionals. Professionals thus embrace 'ideas about management and leadership … seeking new ways to become more organized to ensure legitimacy and sustainability' (Kirkpatrick and Noordegraaf, 2015, p 103). Just as in the case of French business schools, logics appear as important tools for creating legitimacy, opportunistically put to use by professional organizations.

Against this harmonious view, degradation hypothesis proponents would argue that, yes, there are indeed pressures for institutional conformity and in an uncertain world, imitating other organizations is an attractive solution to problems of lost legitimacy, all in line with assumptions from neo-institutional theory (DiMaggio and Powell, 1983). The degradation hypothesis spokesperson would however be hesitant to celebrate this way of increasing legitimacy. Embracing bureaucratic ideals can be a wolf in sheep's clothing. Striving for legitimacy leads to increasing demands of documentation, measurement, and accountability, which in turn lead to increasing administration, and in turn separates the individual professional from her previous control over the evaluation of her work. And once this happens, as sure as that yearly letter from the tax authorities, it leads to increased demands on formalizing the work process in order to make it auditable; degradation has begun. In many cases, the concept of 'professionalism' has been appropriated by bureaucracy and serves as an ideology serving the interest of bureaucracy, thus ironically undermining 'true' professionalism (Evetts, 2003). Professionalism gives a bit of a silver lining and is an attractive identity, perhaps in particular for those in less well-regarded occupations.

The loose couplings hypothesis

In the degradation hypothesis just as the harmony hypothesis, the main idea is that the different institutional logics meet in an organization, and from this conflict or reconciliation develops. In the loose coupling hypothesis, however, the idea is that the logics never quite meet.

The idea with loose couplings is that organizations are not the well-oiled machineries they are thought to be in everyday talk, where the organization is often understood as a set of well-defined roles and relationships, unambiguous division of labour, clear responsibilities, and distinct relations of authority, responsibility, and accountability. The organization relies on plans and strategies and each role is governed by a set of clear job descriptions. Performance measurement and rewards are transparent and objective. We all realize organizations are not like this – but often we assume that this is what they should be, and deviance from this ideal is a problem to be dealt with (Alvehus, 2020). In a machine, loose couplings between the different components cause problems and possibly breakdown.

Organizations, however, are not machines. Too tight coupling causes problems. Taking an example from the paper that popularized the concept (Weick, 1976), think of a school. What goes on in the classroom has little to do with what is decided in strategy discussion in the principal's office, and the principal has very little insight into each teacher's classroom. Also, what happens in the English literature class is not very dependent on what happens in physics class (unless the teachers decide to cooperate). The way in which a teacher chooses to approach a subject will depend not only on a core curriculum but also on personal style and preferences, and the perceived characteristics of the pupils. The student counsellor goes about her or his work without having to care too much about chemistry classes. The quality assurance system is likely mainly a number of forms and reports, produced every year to keep school administration happy. Even centralized grading systems, by their generic nature, always have to be interpreted and adapted to local context: what exactly does 'comprehend' mean in relation to a certain topic, a certain pupil? And so on.

Tightening these connections would cause problems. We would end up in endless coordination efforts, in meticulous form-filling crowding out substantial pedagogical development work. Principals not familiar with the topics of the curriculum or individual pupils would interfere in teachers' pedagogical judgements, likely to a detrimental outcome. Teachers would spend more time coordinating than teaching. Policy makers would hammer out the details of what should be going on in classrooms they had never seen, for pupils they didn't even know existed. And so forth. But, by allowing the different parts of the school machinery to operate independently – but not entirely disconnected – the school as an organization keeps functioning.

This, then, is the essence of the loose coupling hypothesis: Practices based on different institutional logics are separated. When in the school management team, you speak managementese and in the teaching development workshop you speak pedagogese. In the classroom, you talk to pupils. It might frustrate you that these languages do not quite line up, but that is actually the point. At the same time, they are not entirely disconnected (that would be decoupling); they are just loosely coupled.

Thus, lawyers will be able to talk about strategies and quality assurance in the management meeting, but this has little to do with what they actually do with their clients (Winroth, 1999). Reinsurance traders in Lloyd's of London are able to skilfully navigate between different logics by separating them but not entirely compartmentalizing them (Smets et al, 2015). And at the Los Andes, employees were able to balance between the logics of development and banking (Battilana and Dorado, 2010).

But, what then in the loose coupling hypothesis suggests hybridity? It is arguably the fact that the different logics appear in parallel: 'sustainable hybrids and the benefits of their hybridity rely on a system of mechanisms in which individuals continuously enact both the conflict and the interdependence of coexisting logics' (Smets et al, 2015, p 962). The loose coupling hypothesis suggests that the organization is neither entirely balanced, nor dominated by a single logic.

In summary: The degradation hypothesis understands hybridity to be a false, or at least instable, state; the harmony hypothesis suggests hybridity is sustainable and that different logics can harmonize; the loose coupling hypothesis suggest hybridity as an outcome of constant renegotiations between inherently conflicting logics.

We must, at the same time, understand these hypotheses as snapshots. As mentioned, a degradation hypothesis proponent would suggest harmony is unstable and that loose coupling is perhaps a transitory stage; eventually, professionalism sits with the losing hand. Over time an organization may switch between different modes (Smets and Jarzabkowski, 2013). I think most will agree that professionalism is contested terrain and that both professional ideals and professional structures change over time, if slowly. In this long-term perspective, there indeed seems to be evidence for an increasing orientation towards bureaucratic structures, from New Public Management and onwards. But whether this means degradation or a transition to a new professionalism is an open issue that should be settled empirically, on a case-to-case basis.

We're all hybrids now – but we always were

With the previous in mind, it is hard to avoid reflecting on the time dimension in the three hypotheses. This is the reason I chose to draw some several decades old references out of my pocket. The degradation of professional work seems to have been going on for quite some time – at least half a century, but as always we can find examples older than that. But on the other hand, we have yet to see full degradation, so perhaps the process isn't that urgent after all? Or is it that there actually was a point to for example the New Public Management, in that professions before that enjoyed too much autonomy and were no longer accountable to society? And that the development towards professionals internalizing bureaucratic ideals is perhaps not necessarily entirely a negative development, contrary to the degradation hypothesis? As always empirical studies are of interest. In the case of New Public Management, the dominant assessment is that it has had negative impact in various respects, but there is also some evidence to the contrary; see for example Verbeeten and Speklé (2015) and Dan and Pollitt (2015).

And what about new hybrid forms replacing the old professional structure? They were observed by sociologists and organization theorists at least a quarter of a century ago (and as I pointed out in Chapter 2, if we retrofit our theories we can easily find examples in ancient history). Not much new there, either. In fact, one could argue that the very idea that hybridity is something to care about, that it presents a sort of problem, is an outcome of different value spheres having become separated over time – which was Weber's basic idea (1915/1946). The separation of value spheres – and we could make a parallel argument about institutional logics – was for Weber a characteristic of modernity. Church and monarchy being interrelated in the governing of countries in medieval times was not a strange form of hybridity between state and church, between government and faith – it was the nature of things.

This all boils down to what we mean by institutional logics. The hybridity view in the institutional logics literature has a recurring problem in that hybridity entirely exists on the basis of classifications. If – and this is often the case – institutions or institutional logics are understood as representing recurring patterns of action or meaning, different institutional logics must be different such patterns. A hybrid would be a new pattern combining two or more previous ones (as suggested by the first definition of hybrid from Merriam-Webster). But, for how long must a pattern be a pattern before it gains its own box in the classification scheme? Take the case of the 'managerial professional business'. In 1996 this form was understood as increasingly replacing the earlier professional partnership form (Greenwood et al, 1990; Cooper et al, 1996); it is a hybrid in the sense that professional logic here coexists with bureaucratic and commercial logics. Although these papers do not use that label 'hybrid' as they were published before the hybrid hype, the structures they describe would today clearly fall into the category. Most observers would agree that this pattern is now a standard way of managing commercial professional service organizations. It has been around for, then, over a third of a century. The question arises: How long can an observed pattern be 'new enough' to warrant the label 'hybrid'? Should it not be the case that the managerial professional business is an established pattern of recurring action, and as such a very exemplar of an institutional logic – with the lax definitions of institutional logics that often accompany these lines of reasoning – for how to organize professional businesses? And thus, that this hybrid should by now no longer be a hybrid but an established pattern?

I would suggest another route. If we, instead of seeing patterns of behaviour as the core of what institutional logics mean, we can (as I have done in this book) follow the ideal-typical approach of Freidson (2001). If we understand institutional logics to be ideal types and, as such, analytical tools to understand what it is that is going on in organizations, another view opens up. The idea with ideal types, as I noted in Chapter 2, is that they by definition are purely theoretical models. As such, they do not exist as empirical manifestations. In real life, any empirical manifestation will have traces of many ideal types and deviate from the pure form. All organizations will have traces of different logics – and thereby to a different extent struggle with hybridity. Whether such struggles are characterized by conflict or harmony in organizational practice is an empirical question (Greenwood et al, 2011) whereas the analytical viewpoint will merely help us identify potential sites of conflict and need for reconciliation.

This perspective casts the hybridity question in a new light. Professional organizations as hybrids is not something new. In fact, professional organizations, and the organization of professional work, have always been hybrid in the sense that different and conflicting logics are present. A doctor in early 20th century also existed within an economic reality and had to make difficult decisions on what to prioritize in order to make ends meet. Even a small three-person accounting firm (your average Bill, Sue and Jerry's) would need to develop and retain client relationships and secure a stream of income, thereby giving clients some influence over their work, even before turning into a global 'Billsuejerrys' powerhouse. The question shifts from arguing whether the organizations are hybrids or not, towards a question of how the different logics are enacted, and to the balance between them.

Another key concern with concepts of hybridity is that they often seem to confuse the way in which organizations present themselves with the way in which they work. When neo-institutional theory was introduced into organization studies, one key contribution was that there was a need to explain why the image of organizations projected outwards (to clients and other stakeholders) differed from what was going on on the 'inside'. Institutionalized myths about how to organize, how to create accountability, and how to ensure quality abound. It is rational for organizations to seem to live up to these myths in order to gain legitimacy in relationship to their environment. The phenomenon is called institutional isomorphism, and it 'promotes the success and survival of organizations' (Meyer and Rowan, 1977, p 349). Being able to explain what the organization is to its environment is key. Just think about how organizations need to explain their sustainability efforts, their financial performance, their anti-segregation policy, their gender awareness, and so on and so forth.

For organizations operating in complex environments, this means that they need to master institutional isomorphism and hypocrisy (Brunsson, 1989). Hypocrisy – here used as a technical, not derogatory, term – means to say one thing and do another, and often organizations have to do just that in order to fulfil the demands of different stakeholders.

What, then, does this have to do with hybrid professional organizations?

Meyer and Rowan (1977) noted that some organizations can legitimate their existence by unambiguously producing output; in today's terminology we would say that they clearly deliver value. If an organization promises to deliver t-shirts and does so at a low price, its legitimacy is a no-brainer. However, when the organization promises to deliver t-shirts at a low price, while also minimizing environmental impact and providing decent working conditions, the issue becomes trickier. Suddenly there has to be systems of accountability in place to ensure the latter. And this of course opens up for hypocrisy. (Really, who seriously believes that it is possible to produce £1.66 t-shirts without exploiting workers and the environment?)

For professional organizations, the problem explodes. They are saturated with different ambiguities. 'Increasingly, such organizations as schools, research and development units, and governmental bureaucracies use variable, ambiguous technologies to produce outputs that are difficult to appraise … The uncertainties of unpredictable technical contingencies or of adapting to environmental change cannot be resolved on the basis of efficiency' (Meyer and Rowan, 1977, p 354). Professional service organizations exist in a complex institutional environment. Neo-institutional theory suggests, then, that they will develop elaborate structures to live up to conflicting demands – or, then, conflicting institutional logics. This in turn produces ambiguity beyond that of the division of labour in the professional work process. This ambiguity, I will argue in the following, is expressed in the term superficial hybridity.

A fourth hypothesis: superficial hybridity

Working in organizations does not only amount to engaging in the core work. It also means participating in different control activities, and this regards not only managers but also those subject to control (professional stratification, as discussed in Chapter 4, is a good example of this). Whereas neo-institutional theory, just as the earlier-mentioned degradation and harmony hypotheses, approaches institutional processes at an organizational level, issues seem less clear when zooming in on the everyday work. As noted in Chapter 4, control is based on the active participation of those controlled. I think that what happens when we make such a shift in viewpoint largely explains the differences between the hypotheses, and that it also invites an understanding into how all three hypotheses can be correct at the same time. I call this *superficial hybridity*.

In Alvehus (2018) I argued that professional organizations may very well be able to reconcile and sustain conflicting logics and that this reconciliation will look radically different depending on which level of analysis we look at. The study concerns an organization – the tax consultancy that we have met before a couple of times in this book – and its implementation of a new HRM system. The organization committed significant resources to this end. Their aim was explicated very clearly in their mission statement: it was 'to become and be perceived as the best employer in the business in Sweden'. All partners I talked with expressed a genuine belief in this HR initiative and clearly supported it. They wanted to improve the way they were perceived on the 'input market' (a label from Maister, 1993), that is, to presumptive employees, and they wanted to create a more transparent system for performance evaluation that also included 'soft skills', such as business acumen and generosity towards one's colleagues. They aimed at becoming 'less ad hoc' and 'more systematic' in their approach to managing their human resources, and to this end the HR initiative involved the hiring of two HR experts and the appointment of an HR partner.

The new HR system revolved around three areas. First, training. The idea was to develop a more systematic approach to training and development. Previously, this was said to have been mainly about 'learning by doing'. The new system encompassed systematic courses for all employees, to be followed up in the yearly assessment. However, the tax consultants were very sceptical towards this. Two years into the new system, courses certainly had not replaced learning by doing: 'a couple of assignments could easily replace a 20-week university tax course' as one consultant put it (Alvehus, 2018, p 37). On the other hand, the courses were useful for networking. 'Personal networks are everything' (Alvehus, 2018, p 37) one consultant claimed, and to many of the junior employees it also gave a taste of the wider world of the global accounting firm that the tax consultancy department belonged to. In terms of logics, the emphasis was clearly a professional logic, rather than the bureaucratic logic of the HR initiative.

A second area of the HR system was performance measurement. As in many commercial professional service firms, the tax consultancy firm was dominated by billable hours (see Chapter 4). Producing billable hours was a way of unambiguously performing, and billable hours was seen as 'the only tangible communication' and 'you're always guaranteed a bonus based on billable hours' (Alvehus, 2018, p 37). The HR initiative wanted to add soft skills to this, and they developed an elaborate system for assessing such skills, available in a *Personnel Development Handbook*. However, the consultants did not take this system very seriously. The assessment criteria were considered arbitrary and a question of subjective judgement. Many felt they were very much in the hands of their superior. Investing in billable hours made much more sense: That was unambiguous performance with no room for judgement. But this lack of confidence in the system's ability to measure things did not mean that the system was completely ignored. To some extent, a few reasoned, it could be useful, but not for achieving high scores on soft skills, but for developing soft skills in order to increase billable hours.

A third area was a structured approach to personal development. The main idea was to develop a more transparent career path and a sense of feeling for where one was headed in terms of the future in the firm. However, despite all partners being 'in' on the HR initiative, this was a part that was mainly rejected. The general sentiment was not only that your career was in your own hands, but also that the rejection of the HR system itself was a signal. One partner said: 'Taking advantage of opportunities, starting things up, initiating ideas, creating client contacts, marketing yourself; there are no rules for this whatsoever ... I think this is bloody important. In a way, just do it. Do what you want' (Alvehus, 2017, p 39). There was a strong sense of the importance of individualist entrepreneurialism, of finding one's own way and creating one's own future, and to stand out and create one's own image. In this, formal systems such as the HR initiative could actually fulfil an unexpected role: It became something to bypass. By not following the system, it became possible to show independence. For example, despite not being formally allowed to, many junior consultants I met with had developed personal client relations and could thereby themselves control the billing of these clients, creating a lucrative situation in terms of billable hours. And at the same time, they were able to show that they could indeed take on such a responsibility.

So, how can we understand this in terms of institutional logics? On the one hand, there is a case to be made for the harmony hypothesis. The organization, through its partners, invited the bureaucratic HR logic and even invested significant resources into it. They apparently believed that it had some value. On the other hand, the professional logic seemed to dominate, in a sense the opposite of the degradation hypothesis. On the third hand (to the extent that this is a reasonable expression), the two logics sometimes seemed to be reconciled in everyday work. Schematically, we can argue that the bureaucratic logic of HRM was both replicated, revised, and rejected (I here draw on and extend the terminology of Barley and Tolbert, 1997). The area of learning was revised, as attending courses was revised to occasions for networking, but their relevance for learning was rejected as 'learning by doing' dominated. Performance appraisals were replicated by mandatory attendance, but the development of soft skills was revised to being potentially relevant for accumulating billable hours, whereas the valuing of soft skills was explicitly rejected. Finally, the idea of personal development was clearly replicated in the embracing of the overarching HRM ideology, but rejected and even subverted in practice.

Replication occurred at the level of talk and at the level of ritual enactment of performance appraisals (cf Meyer and Rowan, 1977). Some aspects of the HR initiative were useful – courses became occasions for networking, and performance appraisals potentially developed the capacity to generate billable hours – and thus gained a different, revised role. And others yet were outright rejected, and even used for their opposite purpose, as when the HR system for personal development became an example of how not to act.

Hence, superficial hybridity. In a complex world of entangled institutional logics (Alvehus and Andersson, 2018), superficial hybridity is an efficient way of maintaining harmony and conflict simultaneously, and what becomes conflicting and harmonious will be different in different organizations (Greenwood et al, 2011). Logics can be loosely coupled, tightly coupled, and radically reinterpreted all at the same time. It is in the nitty-gritty reality of everyday work we must understand the conflict and reconciliation of institutional logics. A too distanced viewpoint will only reproduce the myths and mystifications produced at the surface. 'True' hybridity perhaps exists only at a distance. It should be noted that superficial hybridity is not about loose coupling. In superficial hybridity, logics – or rather patterns of activities dominated by different logics – are *both* loosely coupled *and* tightly coupled simultaneously, and it allows for replication just as it allows for revision and rejection.

Is the case accounted for here an outlier? I do not think so. Similar phenomena have been observed elsewhere. Pache and Santos (2013) show how organizations can reconcile between logics by cherry-picking some parts of logics and ignoring other; they call it 'selective coupling'. A similar observation is made in health care organizations by Andersson and Liff (2018), who observe how physicians co-opt terminology from different logics to advance their own interests, for example showing how a 'psychiatrist co-opted the managerial logic to support her professional logic by focusing on the division of resources' (p 83) and in a similar fashion Andersson and Gadolin (2020, p 8) show how institutionalized power differences between social categories enable 'physicians' frequent denials to grant influence to any institutional logics other than their own'. Levay and Waks' (2009) notion of 'soft autonomy' captures how professionals become engaged in keeping a distance to external stakeholders in legitimizing their work. At the same time, the same procedures – in this case quality registers – become incorporated into their understanding of how to develop professional quality. An important observation in relation to this is made by Smets and Jarzabkowski (2013). In a study of banking lawyers in a global law firm, they note that whether different logics come in conflict or not is an outcome of how their interrelations are constructed by actors (see also Greenwood et al, 2011). Thus, and as noted in my lengthy account of tax consultants earlier, a case can be made that whereas logics as ideal types are inherently contradictory and conflicting, the way in which this plays out in everyday work is certainly more complex and nuanced.

So, the key take-away from all these studies and others is perhaps the vast variety of outcomes, and seemingly paradoxical outcomes, of interrelations between logics. As explicated in one of the studies just mentioned:

> On the one hand, several professionals appeared to have *internalized* ideas of quality control that originated from outside the healthcare professions and to have embarked on a process that became irreversible. On the other hand, they maintained a significant degree of *control* over important evaluation criteria and thus retained their basic professional autonomy. (Levay and Waks, 2009, pp 520–521, emphasis in original)

Not outright degradation, not harmony, not altogether loosely coupled; instead, parallel processes with different outcomes, and also – as illustrated in the tax consultancy case – different outcomes depending on *where we look*. Hybridity, I suggest, is often superficial and based on observations made at too far a distance. Everyday work is characterized by a constant replication, revision, and rejection of logics.

Redundancy, ambiguity, and superficial hybridity

We can use the notion of bureaucratic and professional logic to shine a light into what it is that is going on. Looking at the tax consultancy case, the ideal types help us see how different logics are reconciled. The patterns could be described as hybrid. But they only seem hybrid from a distanced point of view. Up close the HR initiative rather seems to have crumbled in the face of professionalism. The only place in which the bureaucratic logic remains is on the level of generic talk about the importance of HRM, in the ritualistic performance appraisals, and paradoxically as an exemplar of how to not behave. For all other purposes, the HR initiative is revised or rejected. And similar processes can be observed in other cases.

If patterns of behaviour were inherently contradictory, we would not expect this to happen. Instead, we would find degradation or loose coupling. Here, however, we also find examples of harmonious integration of certain cases, for example in Pache and Santos' (2013) notion of selective coupling.

Remember that second meaning of hybrid? Something with 'two different types of components performing essentially the same function'. In the tax consultancy case, we see exactly that in operation. When it comes to learning and personal development, the professional logic and the bureaucratic logic of the HR initiative aim to accomplish the same thing – they are redundant. And redundancy, despite providing resilience, is not very attractive until the need for that resilience arises. Of course, there were some that found the HR initiative's emphasis on clarity in personal development and learning a good thing, but those were primarily the very junior employees. For them, there was no redundancy – they had not yet been socialized into the profession deep enough to experience that. As Santos (2018) argued, new professionals often appreciate some clarity in the tumultuous ambiguity they experience (see also Chapter 3). Another example is the question of becoming recognized as the best employer in the business. Here, the professional logic offered nothing as it was not something easily projected to outside stakeholders, and again there was no redundancy.

This is what the superficial hybridity thesis suggests: When different logics are redundant, conflict is experienced and processes of reconciliation occur; when logics are complementary, conflict is not experienced. Thus, it may be the case that different institutional logics as manifest in patterns of behaviour are not inherently conflicting; conflict occurs on a case-to-case basis and is constructed in the way different logics become manifest in everyday work. Redundancy in a very concrete sense is a cause of ambiguity that needs to be reconciled, and superficial hybridity describes this complex and open-ended process of reconciliation.

When trying to understand hybrid organizations, and the way in which they operate, we need to do so with a greater sensitivity to local context, that much is clear. Abstracted descriptions have their place, but must always be taken with a grain of salt, in particular if they are limited to discussing public and sweeping representations of organizations. Everyday life is infinitely messier.

7

Understanding the Logic of Professionalism

The aim of this book is to understand the way in which the logic of professionalism is maintained in professional service organizations, taking everyday work as a starting point. In the preceeding chapters, I have explored four topics: the role of ambiguity in professional service work; control over control; the politics of leadership; and superficial hybridity. I have drawn on Freidson (2001)'s typology of market, bureaucracy, and professionalism to highlight the way in which different logics become manifest in everyday work and management. The logics represent different ways of managing work and as should be clear at this stage, a distinct classification of different patterns of activities as belonging to a single logic is a rather futile effort. The main consequence of such an effort is that we zoom out too much and fail to see the way in which agency continuously reshapes patterns of action.

There has over the years been an extensive and sometimes heated discussion about changes in professionalism (often in terms of various threats to professionalism), and about changes in the way in which professional service organizations are managed. The direction and speed at which these changes are happening seems to be more determined by which assumptions about the relationships between logics are held by observers, and at which level of abstraction we look. We are still able to recognize professionalism as a dominant logic in many organizations. Again, this may be due to image work by organizations and occupations trying to obtain or maintain professional status, or it may be due to slowly changing ideas of what professionalism is all about. Yet, it also points towards professional logic being rather resistant to change. The mere fact that we can point to a wide range of organizations, classify them as professional service organizations, and draw clear similarities to organizations of the past, indicates a fairly strong resilience of the professional logic.

Perhaps the question we need to ask is not how professional service organizations change, but why they do *not* change. As I noted in Chapter 2, change is an inherent part of how social practices work. Stability needs to be actively maintained, by for instance formal organizational arrangements. So instead of being surprised that professions, professional jurisdictions, and professional service work change, perhaps we should instead ask: What maintains the logic of professionalism and the coexistence of multiple logics? In the previous chapter I gave one such answer when I suggested the term superficial hybridity to address this. I think, however, that the answer can be qualified a bit more.

When doing this, I will return to the Janus-character of institutional logics I mentioned in Chapter 2. We need to understand both the 'internal and lawful autonomy' (Weber, 1915/1946) of logics, and the way in which actors consciously tweak and transform them in everyday 'core' professional work and in the work of managing professional work. Freidson (2001) aimed to identify what a professional logic is; in this chapter my aim is to identify why professional service organizations persist, and thereby provide an answer to my question of how the logic of professionalism maintains its existence despite the threats posed against it.

I will start this chapter with a brief discussion of a recurring theme in this book, the persistence of ambiguity, that also comprises a summary of the argument so far. Then, I will briefly introduce the idea of latent pattern maintenance. In professional service organizations two such maintenance mechanisms can be identified: functional ambiguity and opaque transparency. I dedicate a section to each, before concluding the chapter with a discussion of the Janus-like character of institutional logics, and the role latent patterns play in maintaining them.

The persistence of ambiguity

Professional service organizations deal with ambiguity, a notion that has been long recognized in studies of professional and knowledge-intensive work (Abbott, 1988; Alvesson, 2001, 2004; Empson, 2017). This observation is central in understanding the relevance of professional logic – as the work and its outcome is ambiguous, it makes sense to allow those who can understand the work and its outcome have control over the work process. Yet, the way in which professional service work is organized, and in particular the way in which division of labour is accomplished, in itself is major cause of ambiguity (see Chapter 3). But there are other factors that generate ambiguity, too.

For example, the way in which different control forms are transformed and even undermined generate ambiguity in how to relate to them, and professional stratification allows professions to retain control over control and thereby maintain the ambiguity in relation to 'outsiders'. This is also strongly related to the division of labour. Control means different things depending on what professional role you find yourself in. Examples include the way in which division of labour relates to stratification, and in the way in which it invites different roles in game-playing.

Leadership is supposedly difficult (the cat-herding metaphor), but in the division of labour there is already a kind of leadership established in master–apprentice roles. This becomes concrete also in the way in which legitimacy is a key component in the leadership dynamics. Collective leadership by itself generates ambiguity in terms of roles, responsibilities, and power constellations. Control forms are, of course, part of the repertoire that individuals in leadership positions wield in the negotiation dynamic, and therefore leadership, management, and control can never be separated. Romanticized images of what leadership should be creates its own form of superficial hybridity, when the 'dirty' politics of everyday life go unacknowledged, and seeming earnest is a central factor in establishing leadership authority.

The notion of superficial hybridity, finally, ties many of the previous threads together. In itself it creates an ambiguous situation in that the relations between different logics are constantly renegotiated and constructed as complementary, conflicting, or whatnot (Greenwood et al, 2011). Superficial hybridity shows the way in which control forms can be present and relevant at the same time as ignored and irrelevant, or even subverted to other purposes. Ambiguity is managed in the division of labour as junior and senior professionals are able to maintain different images of work, sometimes by getting seemingly unsurmountable tasks. Cracking the code of how to relate to different control forms maintains the different ways of relating to them. Leadership and its ambiguous relation to formal structures and the way control and management is subject to negotiation also facilitates both replication and revision of different logics.

Ambiguity is thus constantly produced and reproduced in everyday work and management in professional service organizations. Throughout, the agency present in everyday work comes through strongly. However, much of the agency seems to involve different ways of reproducing aspects of the logic of professionalism. Take for example the ideal of individual autonomy. At the same time as it is maintained, that which the individual has autonomy over seems to sometimes divert from ideal-typical professionalism. Case-centred and client-centred problem solving are both autonomous and subject to division of labour, but client-orientation opens up for a strong element of market logic. Similarly, autonomy plays a part in exploitation within game-playing over time and in tempting insecure overachievers with elite identities.

There is certainly reason to question what it is that is going on in this, and what professionalism means today. I will return to the latter question in the next chapter. In the following, I will dig deeper into the question of what it is that is going on when the logic of professionalism is maintained.

In doing this, I will draw on an idea from Merton (1968), that of latent pattern maintenance. Latent functions, Merton argues, are consequences 'which are neither intended nor recognized' (p 105). In contrast, manifest functions are those 'which are intended and recognized by participants in the system' (p 105). Many such pattern-maintaining processes have been discussed before, in this book and elsewhere. For example, jurisdictional work on behalf of professions is often deliberately intended to maintain professional status (Abbott, 1988), and there are sometimes intentional efforts to challenge aspiring professionals beyond what they see as reasonable and manageable (for example, Kornberger et al, 2011). The sharp distinction between manifest and latent functions is strictly analytical. Of course, there are grey areas, and people can fluctuate between unconsciously reproducing patterns, becoming aware of the consequences of their actions, changing their behaviour and thereby unknowingly reproduce other patterns; the border between our discursive and our practical consciousness is blurry (Giddens, 1984). My purpose in the following is to draw attention primarily to latent pattern maintenance, although it will sometimes overlap with manifest pattern maintenance. I will discuss two different kinds of pattern maintenance going on in professional service organizations: functional ambiguity and opaque transparency.

Functional ambiguity

Instead of seeing ambiguity as something inherent in professional service work that causes certain structures and control forms, I have suggested we see ambiguity as primarily an outcome of specific ways of organizing work. The management of professional service organizations generates ambiguity, and this in turn serves to reinforce the logic of professionalism, in that it maintains autonomy and informal decision-making, and shields the work process from outsiders.

Of course, some ambiguity is hard, if at all possible, to avoid. I call this inherent ambiguity. Whether a certain medical treatment will work in a specific case, or if a contract will actually hold up in court, can never be 100 per cent certain. Sometimes, only the future will tell whether a solution to a professional problem will be a good one. In some instances, we might never know. Perhaps the cancer patient dies in a car accident, or the contract never is stress-tested because no conflicts occur. Or, how should we assess the quality of an education – if the person gets good grades? A high-status job? Lives a rich and rewarding intellectual life? Moreover, applying formal knowledge to client-specific problems calls for judgement and for drawing on one's experience, something commonly not verbalized. This creates ambiguity when searching for words to describe it, but this ambiguity resides in the description and does not necessarily represent profession-relevant ambiguity. Yet, these two aspects provide only a sliver of an answer. In professional training, such talk does occur, and the fact that it does not seem to occur quite so much in talk outside the 'doing' should not be taken as a sign of inherent and persistent ambiguity, but perhaps rather as a sign of inadequate research methods.

But, ambiguity is primarily generated as an outcome of the organization of professional work. In the division of labour, we find it as a core element.

In the model where cases are at the core and clients at the periphery, professionalism is reproduced as the client never gets in contact with case work. There is ambiguity between case work and client work where the profession-relevant ambiguity that the professional is trained to deal with is beyond the reach of the client. The ambiguity of professional work – or at least the image of ambiguity projected 'outward' – is maintained by excluding the client. The societal division of labour between professionals and non-professionals, between laypersons and experts, is therefore reproduced. Ambiguity is functional in the sense that it serves to maintain professional jurisdictions.

In the model where clients are at the core and cases at the periphery, the client is still excluded from case work. Yet here, junior professionals are also excluded from client work. The ambiguity between client work and case work still persists, but now also more clearly in terms of an internal division of labour. The ambiguity is functional in that it maintains a division of labour within the profession and by this reproduces conditions for learning and professional development.

Aspiring professionals' way into the core work, whether client-centred or case-centred, is riddled with ambiguity. They are kept out of client relations, and get tasks they find difficult and almost impossible to deal with. This is a key element in professional training. A fully-fledged professional needs to master the profession-relevant ambiguity, and somehow needs to learn this. Thus, even if it is possible to invite the junior tax consultants to client meetings, not doing so serves as a way of exercising the entrepreneurial muscles of the juniors and preparing them for more responsibilities, and so does demanding seemingly unsurmountable tasks from them. The creation of ambiguity thus has a clear function in this regard. At the same time, it has a function in maintaining economic performance. The division of labour ensures leverage, and the ambiguity becomes a way of assuring that those progressing can maintain their own existence by generating income – the up-or-out system paired with ambiguity is an efficient system for selection. In other cases, the economic aspect might not be quite so prominent. Yet, the functionality in preparing aspiring professionals for managing ambiguities is still there and is reflected in the increasing autonomy, demands, and responsibilities that comes with progression in a formal professional hierarchy.

Another area where ambiguity maintains the professional logic is where professionals maintain ambiguity – often for a good reason – by taking charge over control attempts. As illustrated in Chapter 4, it is not that finding measures for output in professional work is a problem. Billable hours, patients treated, readmittance, and so on – it is not that they are too few, but that they are too many! The problem is that these are not always very relevant indicators, and professions handle this by stratification. In this way, the profession gains strong influence over both the indicators chosen, how they are applied and measured, and how to interpret them. Thus, they take control over control and can maintain a degree of ambiguity. The ambiguity, then, strengthens the profession in that it keeps professionals in control over how to interpret control efforts – and this keeps the fingers of laity and regulators out of the professional cookie jar.

The informal and interpersonal nature of leadership in professional service organizations also produces and maintains ambiguity. Where authority is contingent on professional legitimacy but also on formal bureaucratic hierarchy it is not always easy to answer the question of who it is that is in charge. From a leadership and management perspective, this could seem very dysfunctional. Yet for professional service organizations this ambiguity facilitates efficient decision-making. Participation and involvement take time and this is not always very efficient. Many decisions are made with client considerations in mind and professionals tend to respect this. Political processes are ambiguous and this helps decision-making in that it becomes a way of circumscribing formal authority and instead relies on informal and professionally legitimate authority. Returning to the expectation of cat herding, this imagery in a way legitimates the informal and sometimes inaccessible ways in which decisions get made in professional service organizations.

All in all, these are some examples of the way in which ambiguity is produced by the way professional work is managed, and illustrates how it serves a function in professional service organizations. Ambiguity maintains patterns of action we can understand in terms of professional logic. I call this *functional ambiguity: ambiguity is functional in the sense that it reproduces the conditions for its own existence.* In some cases this will be an outcome of intentional activities (a prime example is deliberately generating obstacles to be overcome by aspiring professionals), but mainly we need to look for the unintended consequences of actions (Giddens, 1984). Functional ambiguity is thus primarily a question of latent pattern maintenance (Merton, 1968). The idea that ambiguity is a core element in the workings of professional service organizations I agree with, but we should not see it as only inherent or as part of the nature of things – it is actively constructed, and this serves the end of maintaining patterns of activity we can understand through the logic of professionalism. I have tried to identify a few such processes.

However, functional ambiguity is but one form of latent pattern maintenance. Another aspect, often ignored in research – possibly due to the interest in ambiguity – is the importance of transparency in maintaining the logic of professionalism.

Opaque transparency

Looking at the previous chapters, it is not only ambiguity that comes through as important for the management of professional service work. In many cases we also see how providing different images of the professional work is important. Such images aim to provide a reasonably unambiguous and transparent image of, for example, a work process or an individual's progression. But the transparency they provide is opaque.

Perhaps the most obvious case I have presented is the way in which time is accounted for in many professional service firms. Basically, the idea is that time can be accounted for straightforwardly: One hour worked means one hour of work is registered. Yet game-playing, ghosting, and the constant self-scrutinization in terms of quality subverts this straightforward transparency. This is very clearly acknowledged in the organizations. In the case of ghosting, it was even brought up as a problem at a meeting studied, yet it persisted. The transparency that could theoretically be there is taken as if it was actually real. This has no small effect: it becomes a way of increasing the real output of the workers without acknowledging it, and together with a work ethic celebrating overwork and the recruitment of insecure overachievers, constructs a situation that can only be described as toxic. The transparency that is provided is opaque and obscures the underlying exploitation and overwork – the system is still seen as functioning in principle; it is the practices that are wrong, yet necessary on a day-to-day basis. It should be pointed out that these examples largely concern extreme contexts. However, we can see traces of the same ideal of transparency also in other contexts, and the extreme cases here help us see that also there, transparency might be opaque and obscure the underlying reality of everyday work.

Models of career paths in HRM systems and the promotion of elite identities are other examples. These are often, by HR experts and new recruits, taken to be clear and transparent descriptions of career stages, the demands connected to them, and what success means. As it turns out, these guidelines mainly seem to provide comfort in a confusing situation. In practice, their role is different. The understanding of how to relate to the formal demands, which ones to focus on and which ones to ignore, and even how to circumvent the system, are more relevant for one's progression. At the same time, formal positions *do* matter as they are related to privileges and responsibilities. The notion of opaque transparency does not mean that the apparent images are not relevant – rather, that they are relevant in a different way than what they imply.

A third example is leadership. Whereas formal positions do have significant impact in the leadership process, key influencers are not always those in formal positions of power. The contingent authority diffuses and obscures the realpolitik of the professional service organization. Imagery is important within the leadership process, too. Appearing earnest, sincere, and as having clear motives are, together with a solid reputation of being able to deliver in the professional work, ways of producing a seemingly transparent image of one's intentions and inner motives, and therefore these are key elements in the power politics of the professional service organization.

Opaque transparency means this: *while a certain way of describing, talking about, or understanding professional service work generates a seemingly transparent image of what it is that is going on, the transparency by itself is opaque and obscures what is actually going on.* When we describe work in terms of the number of hours we have spent on a certain task, we will understand that we have tweaked it by game-playing. But this then becomes an exception, it is not how it is *really* supposed to work. If it was acknowledged that the system of billable hours does in fact work the way it does – game-play, ghosting – it would totally lose its claimed meaning of creating transparency in how much work has been done. Similarly, an HRM system providing a number of 'soft factors' that are estimated at least gives an image of the firm's commitment to their personnel policy and the promotion of work–life balance. Altogether denying the relevance of the HRM system would stain the image of the goodness of the firm. And when management consultants provide rational images of 67-step models for change, when auditors present their sampling models, or when head hunters show the test results of the candidates, denying the relevance of these, or relegating them to being marketing ploys, would likely undermine the legitimacy of the professionals not only in the eyes of their clients – but also in their own eyes.

Yet we must not understand the situation as the professionals being cultural dopes or holding a false consciousness. Many of the examples cited involve a clear reflexivity about how the transparency is not so transparent after all – the discussion on billable hours clearly illustrates this, as does the presence of talk about politics in leadership. The point is, however, that these are often efforts to repair the transparency – they imply that there is something wrong with ghosting or politics, for instance. Seemingly transparent images are thereby effectively maintained as ideals that the organization should live up to, yet it continues to obscure the real workings of the systems.

Maintaining what professionalism?

Institutional logics, understood as ideal types, help us identify and classify patterns of behaviour. Although never appearing in their pure form, logics are ways of making sense of behaviour, highlighting how it reproduces itself in patterns that have some degree of stability. This is one side of the Janus face of institutional logics: the identification of their occurrence, their specific characteristics, and their dynamics – their internal and lawful autonomy (Weber, 1915/1946).

The other side of the Janus face is the patterns of behaviour in everyday life – in this context, work and management in professional service firms. This is fluid, dynamic, and inventive. As I have repeatedly shown, the way in which patterns are interpreted, reproduced, rejected, and revised are manifold (drawing on the terminology in Barley and Tolbert, 1997 and Alvehus et al, 2019a). I do not see any real point in trying to catalogue exactly in which ways, and during which circumstances, they are so – my hunch is that this is largely unpredictable. But, the fact that we can identify something as a recurring pattern of action, and that this has some stability over time and across different contexts, indicates that there are processes making it resilient to change – it is subject to latent pattern maintenance.

Functional ambiguity and opaque transparency both maintain patterns of action that we can identify in terms of the logic of professionalism – they maintain the internal and lawful autonomy of professionalism.

The element in the logic of professionalism that keeps reoccurring is autonomy. As I have tried to show, functional ambiguity and opaque transparency maintain professional autonomy, both on an individual and collective level, and protect it from outside interference. A paradoxical element in this is that division of labour, so key in the professional work process, in fact reveals that few professionals are really that autonomous on an individual level. Aspiring professionals rely on their seniors, and the seniors rely on the assistance of juniors. This doesn't prevent a profession per se from being fairly autonomous; on the contrary, internal divisions of labour and stratification help maintain the profession's autonomy. But this maintaining of professional autonomy does not mean that the content of professional service work is static. Part of the maintenance of professional autonomy is the constant renegotiations of jurisdictions and the struggle for control over control. This is facilitated by the abstract nature of the profession's knowledge base, making it flexible. This also means that within the same profession, we should expect the profession-relevant ambiguity to change over time, and this might even involve switching from case-centred to client-centred problem solving.

The key to professional autonomy, then, lies not in the content of professional work but in the protection of professional autonomy itself. This, protection of professional autonomy at an individual and collective level, is the key element of the logic of professionalism – other aspects are more negotiable and subject to change. We can lament such change, perhaps with a sense of nostalgia for a world lost, but a main insight is that this is not the same as deprofessionalization. Functional ambiguity and opaque transparency ensure the maintenance of the autonomy of the professional logic, despite the fact that the content of the professional work changes.

Professionalism has, I have argued, been able to remain a dominant logic in many organizations. Despite challenges and changes, we can still recognize professional service organizations as a relevant category. This can be explained by the way in which functional ambiguity and opaque transparency protect the professional aspects of work from outside influence, but also in the way they maintain core elements in the way professional work is taught and how professionals are socialized. Partly, these are deliberate strategies, but much of what is discussed here is also a question of unintended outcomes of regular patterns of behaviour that maintain the very same patterns. Interestingly, that which might at first glance seem like behaviour that undermines professional patterns of action by for example engaging in control activities, can in the view presented here be understood as functions that shelter professional logic from being challenged and disrupted by other logics. In the 'fuzzy reality' of the workplace (Abbott, 1988, p 66), functional ambiguity and opaque transparency maintain the internal and lawful autonomy of the logic of professionalism.

8

The Future of Professional Work

In the beginning of this book, I dubbed professionals the gold-collar proletarians of our age. Gold collar, as their work is normally associated with high status and high wages. Proletarians, as it is still wages – the 'free professional' of old is largely an anachronism. At the same time as the status of professions and professional workers is upheld in society, however, 'terminal decline has been a feature of many seminal accounts of the professions and remains influential' (Muzio et al, 2019, p 25). In this book, I have tried to keep to a reasonably non-evaluative view of professionalism. Now of course there is no such thing as a completely value-free social science, but in the context of scholarship on professional service organizations, the problem seems to me that there is sometimes an unnecessary polarization between different camps.

On the one hand we find profession romantics, to whom professionalism is inherently good and the right to secluded professional judgement should always be protected. Control from external stakeholders (clients representing market logic, politicians representing bureaucratic logic, and so on) is from this position always presumed to be negative. In my view, this position blinds itself to the problems inherent in professional monopolies and the power professions hold. Scandals in accounting, in medicine, in finance, and not to speak of the often outrageous and insubstantial claims made by management consultants (a good study to consult [sic!] is Kirkpatrick et al, 2019), should be cause for concern. The much-criticized New Public Management (I have touched upon it occasionally in this book; see Hood, 1991), we must remember, was thought up for good reasons, such as a perceived over-dominance of professions and concerns for ever-increasing costs in for example health care. In short, profession romantics seem to fall prey to the opaque transparency maintaining professional logic. We should also remember that academics are also a profession, and I don't want to point fingers, but it is certainly easier to find comfort in a position that helps to legitimize one's own autonomy. The true cynic would even argue that maintaining theories based on profession romanticism is a key strategy for academics to defend their own jurisdiction. (See also Watson, 2002, who makes a similar observation.)

In the other camp we find the profession sceptics. To them, professionalism involves power abuse and illegitimate claims to expertise, clouded in obscurity. Much of the ambiguities presented in this book are interpreted as self-serving veils of mystification that mainly assist in avoiding insight from politicians, tax payers, and consumers. Professionalism leads to an over-reliance on expertise and thereby undermines democracy as well as individuals' control over their own life. Professions should be scrutinized and preferably their work evaluated systematically, in order to ensure their contribution to society. Seen from my standpoint, this position often involves a naïve view of the possibilities of evaluating professional service work in a relevant way and reducing its ambiguities – it ignores that the transparency of management is incompatible with professionalism (Styhre, 2013). In the logic of professionalism, ambiguity serves important functions. Ambiguity is a key component in how professional development works, and it is endemic in client relationships as clients' needs and problems are in themselves ambiguous in contexts riddled with knowledge asymmetry. Organized professions can fulfil an important societal role by safeguarding quality and ethics in such circumstances.

Arguing that everything in society can be organized according to one logic, whether market, bureaucracy, religion, community, or professionalism, is just as one-eyed as it sounds. But denying belonging to any of these camps doesn't necessarily mean holding a Panglossian view, that everything is as good as it can be. As I stated in Chapter 1, I think that there are reasons to scrutinize professions and professionals, but at the same time, there are values to professionalism that we may want to honour. So somewhere between these two camps, perhaps, lies the future of professionalism. However, the problem with saying anything about the future is that the only thing we know of the future, is that we don't know anything about it. It is a precarious task to discuss what will happen, yet it is of course important. This chapter is not, then, about what professional work is or what it will become, but what it *might* and *could* become.

In the following, I will bring up a number of issues that take me beyond the analysis so far. I extrapolate my line of reasoning into a few, as I see them, key questions. First, I discuss professional logic in relation to market logic in terms of marketization, then in relation to the logic of bureaucracy. The next two sections, on post-truth and technology, deal with challenges to the very heart of professionalism: the legitimacy of knowledge and the role of judgement. In the final section, I discuss how we can retain the values of professionalism.

I also take the liberty of a quite distinct normative position, involving some degree of scepticism against the power of professionals, together with an appreciation for elements of a professional ethos.

The push towards marketization

A common perceived threat to professionalism is increasing marketization: increased emphasis on clients and increased demands for economic performance are understood as pushing in this direction. In terms of institutional logics, this means that market logic is assumed to increasingly supplant professional logic. This is not to say that the logic of the market is the only logic that focuses on clients. On the contrary, as I discussed in Chapter 3, professional problem solving, and therefore the logic of professionalism, at its heart has the interest of clients, sometimes even to the extent that clients' needs come before questions of economic performance (Anderson-Gough et al, 2000). Moreover, this is not only a question at stake in the private for-profit sector. In various public sector reforms, politicians have explicitly sought to import mechanisms from the market into public sector organizations in the welfare sector, of course with varying degrees of success.

However, we should first remember that most professions, just as the guilds that pre-dated them, have always lived under economic conditions and sometimes in directly competitive situations. Even if a guild or profession gains monopoly over a certain set of tasks, we still find intra-professional competition, and at the very least, the professional worker needs to find a decent income. It's is easy to let nostalgia take a hold here. For instance, pre-Second World War US medicine was largely a 'cottage industry' comprised of independent doctors and financed by charities and patients themselves (Freidson, 1985). Yet, imagining that these physicians were free from economic pressure would be a mistake. At the end of the day, they depended on their patients and the charities in order to make ends meet. (And to this we can add other significant issues such as inequality, class, and access to health care.)

The accounting profession can serve as an example. An increased market orientation is sometimes argued to lie behind decreasing ethics in accounting firms. This is in turn assumed to catalyze high-profile scandals involving fraud, forgery, and money laundering. The Wikipedia page for 'Accounting scandals' lists 64 such major scandals since 2000.[1] Even before major public scandals such as Enron (in 2001) and the following demise of global

---

[1]   See https://en.wikipedia.org/wiki/Accounting_scandals (accessed 15 January 2021).

accounting firm Arthur Andersen, or Lehman Brothers (in 2010) involving Ernst & Young, the accounting profession was questioned due to its increased market orientation. Hanlon (1996) discussed the rise of a commercialized service class replacing traditional professional concerns, and the managerial professional business was understood as replacing the traditional professional service firm (Cooper et al, 1996). In theoretical terms we can see this as an argument that such firms are increasingly dominated by a market logic, although professional failure in general can of course not be reduced to marketization alone (Muzio et al, 2016).

But there are also dimensions to the logic of professionalism that drive increasing demands for economic performance and market expansion. The up-or-out system, described in Chapter 4, is strongly rooted in the logic of professionalism, yet it also needs economic performance in order to expand, and expansion is, in turn, key for the up-or-out logic to function as an efficient incentive system. Without expansion it turns into an, in terms of incentives, less efficient dead man's shoes system (Baden-Fuller and Bateson, 1990). It is therefore far too easy to associate economic performance with market logic – it is also inherent to at least some versions of the logic of professionalism, based on leverage grounded in division of labour combined with up-or-out career systems. Perhaps growth legitimized in traditional professional division of labour is as much of a problem as market orientation per se? When talking to senior partners in professional service firms I often get the impression that the best days in their professional lives were when they were still working in a small firm. Is it just nostalgia, or is it so that something important gets lost in growth?

My argument in relation to the marketization of professional service organizations, then, is that we need to see this as an increased tendency towards superficial hybridity. The logic of professionalism still seems able to retain professional autonomy, while other professional ideals are seemingly sacrificed and more market-oriented aspects become more prominent. This is of course more likely to happen in client-centred professional work than case-centred. Increasing client orientation may not necessarily lead to the decrease of professional logic, but it does shift the content of professional work in a more commercial orientation. It shows the opaque transparency in operation, maintaining professional autonomy.

One potential development that should be noted lies somewhat outside the professional service organization context, and this is the development towards a professional gig-economy. To the extent that the demand for professional services increasingly go towards standardization, not least with the help of technology (see the section 'Technological dreams and nightmares'), a possible development is the one described by Barley and Kunda's (2004) study of freelance technical contractors: fierce price competition and a thorough financialization of every aspect of life, where the workers constantly have to decide whether to invest in work, training, marketing, or undertaking work for clients – not unlike the financialization of billable hours systems. Accounting, to continue with the earlier example, is particularly susceptible to this as it largely is a standardized service. Freelancing apps for standardized professional services can potentially challenge the professional logic of large professional service organizations and push for an increased market logic, at least for small- and medium-sized clients. If, and how, professions will respond to this, and how they can mobilize to retain their status, their jurisdiction, and avoid a race to the bottom in terms of income, will be interesting to see. But if technology makes it increasingly difficult to maintain the opaque transparency and the functional ambiguity in professional training is challenged by artificial intelligence, we must also ask from a consumer perspective: do we actually need professions?

The Trojan horse of bureaucracy

The main character of professional logic is oriented towards maintaining autonomy, both at an individual and collective level. Yet, this means that work practices may become susceptible to various forms of rationalization and standardization. For example, through the functional ambiguity keeping junior professionals out of client relations, tax lawyers are able to sustain a part of the workforce that delivers cheap labour, achieving leverage – thereby starting to orient their work towards a market logic. When the collective protects its jurisdictions by starting to live up to external standards, this may also affect the core work. In health care and in teaching, we find professionals turning to elite roles and thereby, with a high degree of legitimacy, contributing to increased controls and to some extent increased standardization within the core work of the profession at the demands of external stakeholders – increasing the bureaucratic logic in the name of professionalism.

Growth, brought up in the previous section, is almost always associated with increased bureaucracy and demands for routinization (Mintzberg, 1979; Kärreman et al, 2002). This is sometimes – perhaps due to the romantic belief in leadership as a distinct competence – accompanied by professional service organizations hiring non-profession managers. Empson (2017) illustrates how increased size and internationalization seems to go hand in hand with demands for a more 'professional' management – which in context means strengthening bureaucratic logic, not professional logic. To some extent the logics of market and bureaucracy launch a coordinated attack on professionalism. In such cases, there is of course a risk that professionals lose the control over control that is otherwise handled by stratification. We can see a shift in logics when non-professionals (clients and managers) instead of professional workers increasingly exert influence over work. Together with increasing administration this likely leads to redundancy in functions and thereby to conflicts between logics.

A common mistake is to view professionals as the only agents in this process, and administration as an anonymous external force. This is, of course, not the case. On the contrary, administrators also represent occupational groups, sometimes with professional aspirations (for example human resource management expertise), and as such are players in the struggle for jurisdiction (Alvehus, 2019a). We must see to their agency in this process, too. They may have their own abstract knowledge base, for example in 'core values work', 'coaching', or 'personnel development', practices often supported and legitimized through their presence as topics for study at universities. When professionals have increasingly recruited administrative personnel to manage not only the administration generated by the professionals' work, but also part of the control over control, this may indeed be a Trojan horse. Even if the professional core work remains unaffected, the professionals will increasingly have to take part in various kind of activities not related to their core work. As I noted in Chapter 4, control demands participation of those controlled and, therefore, control activities can start competing with the core professional work for attention and cause a crowding-out effect or intensification of the overall work situation.

Another key issue to be dealt with is stratification. I have previously shown how this, by opaque transparency, helps maintain professional autonomy. However, we must at the same time question what administratively oriented elite professionals actually accomplish. To some extent demands for, for example, transparency may help in holding professionals accountable and maintain standards of quality – and as far as this is the case, it should probably be understood as a positive development. However, much is about living up to standards and norms that have very little to do with the content of the core professional work. We should always ask whether another plan or policy regarding equality, sustainability, or core values actually accomplishes much in practice, other than drawing time and energy from those participating in its implementation and realization. These kind of window-dressing activities (Alvesson, 2013) are rarely beneficial to anyone except those working with developing them.

There are strong reasons to see these tendencies as real. Despite professions per se being able to survive, this is not necessarily the same as professionalism remaining the same. To some extent, these developments can have positive outcomes – remember the anecdote about the Formula One team (Chapter 4). But, as noted by some, this might in the long run undermine the space for individual autonomy and judgement in professional work. Several observers have noted how professional values increasingly merge with bureaucracy, sometimes at the professionals' own initiative (Kirkpatrick and Noordegraaf, 2015). Managerial discourses enter the professional vocabulary and slowly, almost imperceptibly, transform it, driving the development towards 'organizational professionalism' (Evetts, 2011), where the values of professionalism is all in the hands of the bureaucracy. Professional logic maintains individual professional autonomy but there are reasons to believe that this is not always synonymous with autonomy in relation to the bureaucratic organization through a professional collective. Professionalism becomes hijacked or slowly erodes (Bejerot and Hasselbladh, 2011). Thus, paradoxically, professional work might actually become corrupted by the very attempts to protect it.

It is here that traditional professionalism, with its values, slowly might give way to other logics. We must then, again, remember what it is that these institutional logics help us see: Who controls work? Is it controlled by individuals or collectives of professionals, or by a formal managerial hierarchy (populated by professionals or non-professionals)? Is it the clients' needs as perceived by the professional that dominate, or the clients' needs as expressed in terms of demand on the market? These are the key issues, and from this perspective, some traditional professions such as accounting might be on the verge of becoming professions in name, self-identity, and status only. The problem is that seeing this is often obscured by opaque transparency – especially as long as we hold on to the ambiguity assumption in studies of professional service work.

Control is to some extent both pointless and counter-productive. Pointless in the sense that professionals will take control over control systems, and counter-productive in the sense that this causes work efforts to be directed towards maintaining opaque transparency instead of doing the professional work. For the profession this may be a worthwhile 'investment' as it protects its jurisdictions and interests, but from a societal point of view it is likely best viewed as a waste of resources.

Whether professionalism is really under threat from bureaucratic or market logic must always be an empirical question, and it should be determined by close-up empirical studies of professional service work, in situ. We need to understand institutional changes at the coalface (Barley, 2008), taking the complexities and power dynamics of everyday professional work and managerial work into account. There are such studies, but all too few. Moreover, in this we must retain an analytical distinction between different institutional logics and an awareness of how they are maintained, as well as the insight that rationalization and changing jurisdictions are not automatically equivalent to deprofessionalization.

Expertise in post-truth society

At the heart of professionalism we find, ideal-typically, an established knowledge base legitimated by science. It is from this, for example, that key parts of the Hippocratic oath become meaningful. In one modern version of the oath, we find the following: 'I will respect the hard-won scientific gains of those physicians in whose steps I walk, and gladly share such knowledge as is mine with those who are to follow.'[2] Incorporating and sharing scientific knowledge is an indispensable element.

Today, however, some argue that we live in a post-truth society, meaning that lay persons increasingly question science and established expertise, simply because they choose not to believe things that go against their viewpoints, whether grounded in religion, political ideologies, or plain conspiracy theories: 'post-truth is not so much a claim that truth *does not exist* as that *facts are subordinate to our political point of view*' (McIntyre, 2018, p 11, emphasis in original). In short, a worldview becomes resistant to facts that displease, sometimes called 'knowledge resistance' (Klintman, 2019). Questions such as these of course raise classic epistemological questions – what does it mean to 'know' something? – but more importantly the post-truth condition also means that facts of which we can be reasonably sure are for some supplanted by hocus pocus and pseudo-science; the anti-vaxxer movement comes to mind. This is fuelled not only by celebrities peddling snake oil, but has also been established as a key strategy for companies in the tobacco, oil, and other industries, where undermining scientific legitimacy is established business practice (Proctor, 2008; McIntyre, 2018). In a world where nothing is true, everything becomes possible, to paraphrase Russian journalist Peter Pomerantsev (2014).

These trends are, however, to some extent something that is more important in the political sphere than in professionalism, although, for example, physicians might find themselves questioned by more informed as well as more misinformed, yet certain, clients. But professionalism has its own problem with what exactly constitutes a legitimate knowledge base. Professional problem solving involves the application of abstract expert knowledge to clients' problems (Abbott, 1988; Empson et al, 2015a). This expertise is based on a knowledge asymmetry between professionals and clients, but also on a trust that the professionals actually deliver something important, something of value.

Some occupations operating as professionals are, however, borderline cases in this regard. Much leadership and management consultancy, for

---

[2]   See https://en.wikipedia.org/wiki/Hippocratic_Oath (accessed 16 January 2021).

example, keep selling services based on 'n-step' models of organizational change (Alvesson and Sveningsson, 2008) or models of 'transformative' and 'situational' leadership, despite such models having been thoroughly questioned by research. Experts in recruitment often use personality tests that have no scientific validity whatsoever.[3] And so on. As Clark (1995) argues, these are mere props that sustain a performance, creating images and providing legitimacy. Such firms, then, ride high on the opaque transparency, relying on the clients' willing participation. We must avoid, however, seeing clients as duped. As argued by, for example, Sturdy (1997), the power dynamics are more intricate and interactive. Consultants are often as much in the hands of clients as the opposite is the case, which means that market logic certainly plays a part here, and in order to understand this we again need to move towards studying these processes at the coalface. There is a supply and demand for these services (Abrahamsson, 1996), meaning that they are based on interaction between service provider and client.

An illustrative case is the notion of value-based health care, a concept marketed by, among others, Boston Consulting Group (BCG). Investigative journalists Gustafsson and Röstlund (2019) account for how when rebuilding the Nya Karolinska Solna (NKS) hospital in Sweden, consultants were involved at an early stage, with the idea to completely redesign the health-care processes. Their models were convincing and supported by high-profile academics, and political decision-makers were persuaded. In the change, the medical profession was effectively excluded from decision-making processes and their opinions were ignored. For example, much of the heart of the design of the new workflows were ill-matched to reality. They were oriented towards single diagnosis, whereas multi-diagnosis patients comprised the absolute majority. The value-based care was consumer value-oriented rather than founded on professional judgement, and processes were organized according to ideas from the manufacturing industry, ill-suited for health-care realities at a large hospital. The outcome was a dysfunctional and very expensive hospital, but of course, BGC made a healthy profit on the way; between 2010 and 2017 NKS had consultancy costs of over 1 billion SEK (over €100 million) of which about a quarter went to BCG (other major firms such as Ernst & Young were also engaged). BCG do not market their ideas under the label value-based health care in Sweden any longer, but the ideas are not dead.

The case of NKS is perhaps an outlier but it is not unique. A large quantitative study of the British National Health Service found that investment

---

[3]   The highly popular Myers-Briggs test is, for example, highly questionable. A good and accessible discussion can be found here: www.vox.com/2014/7/15/5881947/myers-briggs-personality-test-meaningless (accessed 14 January 2021).

in management consultancy is related to increased *in*efficiency: 'Contrary to the claims made by clients, consulting firms and their representative bodies, management consultants are not significantly improving the efficiency of NHS organisations' (Kirkpatrick et al, 2019, p 91). This should be a wake-up call for knowledge-resistant decision-makers and in terms of professionalism it should lead to a serious questioning of the knowledge claims these autonomy-maintaining professions actually make. Managers and decision-makers live with performance pressures and expectations of change, and consultants providing solutions backed by brands and legitimacy, guided by norms of progress and technical efficiency (Abrahamsson, 1996), bring simplistic and easy-to-digest solutions to complex problems, thereby reducing anxiety for their clients.

Some argue that professions increasingly depend on developing connections with extra-professionals and that we are moving, therefore, towards a 'connective professionalism', a view of professionalism that argues that 'professionalism is not "made" by professionals themselves, but dependent upon many actors and factors in broader service processes and wider service ecologies' (Noordegraaf, 2020, p 219). However, and as noted by others (for example Adams et al, 2020), professions, insofar they exist as unified bodies, have always been constituted relationally. Even though they may appear as autonomous entities their exclusivity was built on opaque transparency enacted in relations. Yet we should also acknowledge that there are societal trends here that increasingly call expertise into question, for good or for bad. Perhaps the issue is not so much whether professions are becoming increasingly connective. Instead we need to ask questions such as: What relationships are becoming important? How does the character of those relationships shift when moving from a case-based to a client-based work model? Can opaque transparency be maintained and retained as legitimate in a post-truth world, and if so, how? In many ways, the changes identified by for example Noordegraaf (2020) might primarily be novel ways of maintaining functional ambiguity and opaque transparency (Alvehus et al, 2021).

Technological dreams and nightmares

Technology is always enmeshed with fantasy. We live in revolutionary times – always. A gaze back into history reveals the machine age, the atomic age, the space age, service society, knowledge society, IT-society, post-Fordist society, the information age ... all in the last one hundred years. We seem to have a constant need of seeing contemporary society as being at a turning point: 'Now, everything changes!' Technology is claimed to be a key component of this sense of continuous revolution. Once it was the machines of the industrial age, today it is the 'age of the smart machines' (Zuboff, 1988), the latest fuss being artificial intelligence (AI), deep learning, machine learning, big data, and quantum computing. Brynjolfsson and McAfee (2014) argued for the coming of 'the second machine age', Tegmark (2017) for 'life 3.0', and Zuboff (2019) for the 'age of surveillance capitalism'. Utopic or dystopic imagery dominates; disruption is the word on (almost) everyone's tongue.

When it comes to professional service work, the changes are presumed to be no less revolutionary. Susskind and Susskind (2015), in the perhaps most extensive discussion to date, argued that due to these technological developments,

> the professions will undergo two parallel sets of changes. The first will be dominated by automation. Traditional ways of working will be streamlined and optimized through the application of technology. The second will be dominated by innovation. Increasingly capable systems will transform the work of professionals, giving birth to new ways of sharing practical expertise. (Susskind and Susskind, 2015, p 271)

Disruptive and revolutionary changes, indeed. And undoubtedly, such changes have transformed other businesses. My grandfather was a carpenter, and I cannot imagine that when he went about his business in the Swedish Småland forests in the 1950s, he could foresee the way in which standardized, large-scale, non-craft production of furniture would come to dominate the market in a few decades – driven by a company, Ikea, founded just over 150 kilometres from where he lived and worked. The impact has been profound.

Yet, we have also seen technological changes in other areas, where the impact has been less dramatic for professionals. Medicine would be one example. Medical technology has developed dramatically over the last few decades. This has of course changed the work within the medical professions, and it has changed the jurisdictions between different specializations and sub-professions. Yet it has not led to the demise of the medical profession. As Abbott's (1988) model suggests, professions survive by changing their jurisdictions. Automation and innovation changes jurisdictions and thereby what professionals do, but they do not automatically obliterate professions or deprofessionalize workers.

Currently, however, the seemingly ever-increasing speed of technological development is considered by many a fundamental threat to professionalism. In a report that gained international recognition, Frey and Osborne (2013) concluded that 'recent developments in [machine learning] will put a substantial share of employment, across a wide range of occupations, at risk in the near future' (p 39). Their analysis builds on task analysis, identifying those jobs that are more susceptible to computerization and robotization. Notably, it is not only routine tasks that are possible targets for automation. What is called 'Moravec's paradox', from robotic engineer Hans Moravec, means that while we traditionally may have assumed that simple mechanical tasks were easier to replace by robots, it is in fact easier to replace intellectual tasks (Brynjolfsson and McAfee, 2014). Machines easily beat us in chess, Jeopardy and Go, but it is still difficult to design a robot to feed soup to a person suffering from Parkinson's disease in a dignified way. Many intellectual tasks are under threat of being replaced by machines, Frey and Osborne therefore argued. In legal work, for example:

> paralegals and legal assistants – for which computers already substitute – [are] in the high risk category. At the same time, lawyers, which rely on labour input from legal assistants, are in the low risk category. Thus, for the work of lawyers to be fully automated, engineering bottlenecks to creative and social intelligence will need to be overcome, implying that the computerisation of legal research will complement the work of lawyers in the medium term. (Frey and Osborne, 2013, p 41)

From a profession perspective, one key observation should be made here. As this analysis concerns tasks, we must take into consideration the way in which professions' flexible knowledge base and changing jurisdictions can meet this.

Law in an interesting case-in-point. This profession stands, some say, before an 'unprecedented upheaval' (Susskind and Susskind, 2015, p 67) with the coming of standardization, databases, and automated systems. The question, however, is to what extent this is a threat to the profession per se, or whether it means that new divisions of labour and jurisdictions will develop within the legal profession and between lawyers and other service providers. Law, and other professions, seem more to verge towards 'AI-enabled' than being replaced entirely (Armour and Sako, 2020). Lawyers may very well be able to use computer assistance instead of human assistants, but this does not mean that the legal profession per se will be threatened – the way its division of labour works will, and the task jurisdictions will. And perhaps the size of the legal profession. Possibly, new competencies need to be brought in to develop the new work, but again this does not mean that the profession becomes less professional, it means that the work changes. What these predictions then say is that law as a profession will change – not necessarily that it will disappear, or that it will become deprofessionalized.

Observations in line with this have been made in law firms. In a recent study, Kronblad (2020) argues that law firms are undergoing changes due to digitalization. Notably these mainly seem to derive from increased pressure from clients to provide on-the-spot, cheap legal solutions. Some of this might be facilitated by technology, but the technology per se plays only one part. This has impact on the way to do business, as when some 'of the work that junior associates did in the past is replaced by technology', this encourages the firms to develop new models for pricing including 'an increase in fixed prices, subscriptions, and value-based models' (Kronblad, 2020, p 450). However, what we see here is not deprofessionalization, but a change from one market logic business model (billable hours) to another (fixed prices, subscriptions). Whether this impacts on professional autonomy remains to be seen, but it is at least not a straightforward determinate process. The main impact in terms of the work process seems to be the way in which routine work can be handled by machines instead of a cadre of junior lawyers – a kind of development familiar in the history of many professions, when tasks that become routine enforce changes in jurisdictions.

What is of interest, however, is the way in which these potential changes will affect the professional division of labour, and in particular the role that functional ambiguity plays in professional development. This was raised by an accountant I met at a convention in London some years ago, and he was very concerned about the socialization of new accountants. And, of course, also about the possibility of maintaining the leverage-based business model in the future. ('Wallet issues' matter!) Large-scale AI and machine learning applications in tasks that have traditionally been handled by junior professionals in client-centred division of labour threatens the leverage on which these firms rely. It also puts to the professionals the question of how to train and develop new recruits. This might be of some concern to a single organization, but it is an even greater issue for professions per se if the ways of developing professionals no longer are part of a profit-generating system.

Another issue is the quality of work. Given that we have a situation characterized by knowledge asymmetry (Sharma, 1997), who will be able to tell whether the automated systems deliver the same quality as human professionals would? This is in fact one possible route for professional stratification: a further development of 'evidence-based' controls and of auditing algorithms in order to secure quality.

Agreeing with Lester (2020), I would therefore argue that the changes we see now primarily imply

> occupational transformation, with implications for both initial education and reskilling. Importantly, many professional occupations will be affected directly by automation and substitution, with human expertise becoming less essential for even some highly complex tasks. This does not, however, spell mass redundancy across these occupations, but it will see changes to the tasks, fundamental skills and modes of organising of practitioners. (Lester, 2020, p 11)

In many cases, the 'core' of professional work will shift, but the professions will remain. We may see a move towards structures such as those in traditional industries, observed by Woodward (1965), where the workflow is maintained by automated labour (machines), overwatched by a highly skilled workforce (professionals). This shift might be more dramatic for client-oriented firms that rely on the traditional leverage model for profit-generation, but will likely leave none untouched. The processes maintaining the autonomy are strong, and a reasonable development is that professions incorporate the new technologies into their jurisdiction.

In the times that lie ahead, we can expect new forms of professionalism and the deprofessionalization of specific tasks – but likely not, at least in the foreseeable future, the demise or disappearance of professions. Changes in the labour market seem in fact to be much less dramatic than either the utopians or dystopians suggest. As put by Rolandsson et al (2020), 'the spectre of massive digital job destruction has not materialized' (p 84).

Professions have always been changing and likely will continue to. The deprofessionalization argument seems mainly driven by either a failure to recognize this, or by a form of nostalgia. However, to the extent that new technologies facilitate higher performance at lower cost I personally see little need for such nostalgia. If for example medical technology would develop to the point that I can get an accurate diagnosis from a tricorder (Star Trek) and heal my lightsabre wounds in a bacta tank (Star Wars), I certainly would not be the one to object.

In defence of professionalism as value

Power over work means power over what most adults are expected to do for at least a third of their day. Time, and the choice of what to do with it, is what we have in this life (Hägglund, 2019). Power over work means power over life.

In the beginning of this book, I argued that we need to understand professionalism in the context of the last 50 or so years' emphasis on knowledge as a key factor of production in society. A key factor of production, we can expect, will be under pressure for efficiency in a competitive economy, and from governments' and taxpayers' wish for the efficient use of public funds. Is the loss of professionalism inevitable, does an 'irresistible tide' (Krause, 1996, p 286) of capitalism and state power eradicate the values of professionalism – autonomy, client orientation, and so on? Perhaps ideals of transparency and control, embodied in the logic of bureaucracy, erode professionalism in the long run (Styhre, 2013)? Perhaps professionalism, close to the ideal type, is today an impossibility to the extent that the ideal type becomes rather meaningless for understanding how work is undertaken. Or, can we find dignity of work in a society where even the intellectual aspects of work are being brought under the yoke of industrial mass production and automation?

Perhaps we can.

The logic of professionalism, I argued in Chapter 7, seems very efficient in maintaining its internal and lawful autonomy, where the key element is individual and collective autonomy. Functional ambiguity and opaque transparency play key parts in this. As I have argued in this chapter, we see professionalism under threat today, not in maintaining its autonomy, but in maintaining its values. Marketization and commercialization is a strong incentive system paired with professional division of labour, and stratification to meet demands from bureaucratic logic takes professional work further from its core. Participating in activities and keeping control over control leads to a crowding out of what the professional work was about in the first place. Technology might even, with advances in AI and machine learning, erode the role of inference work. On the other hand, to the extent that this all actually achieves more transparency, it might actually prevent some of the unwanted consequences of relying on trust – over-reliance on expertise, lack of insight (in particular relevant for the public sector), and professions losing their moral compass. Professions are by no means free from guilt when it comes to fraud or even partaking in atrocities such as unethical medical experiments. Seclusion and an unquestioning attitude – from the public, politicians, shareholders, and researchers – is not a workable way forward.

There is thus a paradox involved in the maintenance of professionalism. By trying to manage and control professional work from a bureaucratic or market logic, key aspects of professionalism are being eroded. The consequence is a retained strength of professional logic but more work and effort being put into activities maintaining opaque transparency. It takes professions further away from that which constitutes their core legitimacy – judgement-based work based on expert knowledge that demands trust from society. What is in danger is not professions or the autonomy-generating logic of professionalism, but the very values this was meant to secure in the first place.

But the values that professionalism is ideal-typically concerned with are still important. Many tasks in society still depend on professional judgement, often involving compassion for clients and an ability to place work in a broader societal and moral context. To the extent that this is in fact undermined by bureaucracy and management, trying to manage professional work by logics other than that of professionalism, such efforts must be seen as counter-productive.

Is there a way out of this seemingly deadlocked situation? Perhaps. Just as craft work, professional work has elements that should be embraced in order to encourage a more humane and dignified working life: pride in one's work, pride in one's development, reflection, sharing of knowledge, and imagination (Sennett, 2008). Organizing work in a way where the clients' needs become something more than billable hours and not confined to inference only. Realizing that judgement takes time, not only in work processes but also in that it takes time to develop. Seeing ambiguity as a productive part of meaningful apprenticeship. Understanding that increased controls do not necessarily produce better output, and often accomplishes the opposite. Any decision-maker wanting to impose a new control system should first ask themselves: Would I become more satisfied, motivated, and efficient if I myself was subjected to this system? Most of the time, the answer will be no. That should be a red flag.

But trust in judgement demands responsibility. We – the recipients of the outcome of professional work – must maintain meaningful standards of performance. The transparency must be of a certain kind: 'the standards of good work must be clear to people who are not themselves experts' (Sennett, 2008, p 249). A reflexive, critical, and educated approach to control – why not supported by competent 'grey hair' ex-professionals? – is needed, because professionals are certainly *not* best left entirely to their own devices. This must not, however, mean adding new control dimensions. Primarily it means removing many external controls, reducing the demand for 'transformative' and suchlike leadership, and allowing the management inherent in the logic of professionalism do its job. This might be experienced as a loss of control for top management and stakeholders – but as a comfort, the control they lose will largely be that of opaque transparency.

Perhaps professions need to disassociate from professional service organizations, involving a significant power shift. This would include professional associations reclaiming responsibility for developing systems for judging professional competence and career steps, thereby advocating meritocracy rather than interpersonal up-or-out competition as the foundation for career progress. Yet another step – that certainly goes against market orientation – is to set salary standards for professionals, tied to career steps, thereby deliberately undermining the power of the employing organization and shifting the loyalty of the professional from the organization to the profession.

The personal ethos of craftsmanship and professional work is a value we need to retain. This value is not strengthened by either market or bureaucratic logic, but by strengthening those aspects of professionalism that amount to other things than producing only opaque transparency and functional ambiguity. We must value the heart of professional work – the heart understood both as the core work, and as the cognitive and emotional commitment towards a greater good.

References

Abbott, A. (1988). *The System of Professions*. Chicago: University of Chicago Press.

Abbott, A. (1991). The future of professions: Occupation and expertise in the age of organization. *Research in the Sociology of Organizations*, 8(1), 17–42.

Abrahamsson, E. (1996). Management fashion. *Academy of Management Review*, 21(1), 254–285.

Adams, T.L., Kirkpatrick, I., Tolbert, P.S., and Waring, J. (2020). From protective to connective professionalism: Quo vadis professional exclusivity? *Journal of Professions and Organization*, 7(2), 234–245.

Alexius, S. and Furusten, S. (2019). Exploring constitutional hybridity. In S. Alexius and S. Furusten (eds), *Managing Hybrid Organizations: Governance, Professionalism and Regulation* (pp 1–25). Cham: Palgrave Macmillan.

Alford, R.R. and Friedland, R. (1985). *Powers of Theory: Capitalism, the State, and Democracy*. Cambridge: Cambridge University Press.

Alvehus, J. (2012). *4 myter om professionella organisationer*. Lund: Studentlitteratur.

Alvehus, J. (2017). Clients and cases: Ambiguity and the division of labour in professional service firms. *Baltic Journal of Management*, 12(4), 408–426.

Alvehus, J. (2018). Conflicting logics? The role of HRM in a professional service firm. *Human Resource Management Journal*, 28(1), 31–44.

Alvehus, J. (2019a) Administrationens expansion som professionaliserings-process: En idéskiss. In *Ökande administration – Belägg och potentiella förklaringar: två essäer*. KFi Rapport nr 155. Göteborg: Göteborgs universitet.

Alvehus, J. (2019b). Emergent, distributed, and orchestrated: Understanding leadership through frame analysis. *Leadership*, 15(5), 535–554.

Alvehus, J. (2020). En blick in i det företagsekonomiska tänkandets grundläggande struktur. In J. Alvehus and D. Ericsson (eds), *Om undran inför företagsekonomin*. Stockholm: Santérus.

Alvehus, J. (2021). Docility, obedience and discipline: Towards dirtier leadership studies. *Journal of Change Management: Reframing Leadership and Organizational Practice*, 21(1), 120–132.

Alvehus, J. and Andersson, T. (2018). A new professional landscape: Entangled institutional logics in two Swedish welfare professions. *Nordic Journal of Working Life Studies*, 8(3), 91–109.

Alvehus, J., Avnoon, N. and Oliver, A.L. (2021). 'It's complicated': Professional opacity, duality and ambiguity. A response to Noordegraaf (2020). *Journal of Professions and Organizations*, Online.

Alvehus, J. and Crevani, L. (forthcoming). Micro-ethnography: An approach for doing multimodal leadership studies. Under review for *Journal of Change Management: Reframing Leadership and Organizational Practice*.

Alvehus, J. and Hallonsten, O. (forthcoming). Institutional logics as a functionalist differentiation theory: A (re)interpretation of the sociological roots. Under review for *Organization Theory*.

Alvehus, J. and Kärreman, D. (2019). Kunskapsorganisationer och kunskapsarbete. In S. Sveningsson and M. Alvesson (eds), *Organisationer, ledning och processer* (3rd edn, pp 395–419). Lund: Studentlitteratur.

Alvehus, J. and Spicer, A. (2012). Financialization as a strategy of workplace control in professional service firms. *Critical Perspectives on Accounting*, 23(7–8), 497–510.

Alvehus, J., Eklund, S., and Kastberg, G. (2019a). Inhabiting institutions: Shaping the first teacher role in Swedish schools. *Journal of Professions and Organization*, 6(1), 33–48.

Alvehus, J., Eklund, S., and Kastberg, G. (2019b). *Lärarkåren och förstelärarna. Splittrad, stärkt och styrd profession*. Lund: Studentlitteratur.

Alvehus, J., Eklund, S., and Kastberg, G. (2020). Organizing professionalism: New elites, stratification and division of labor. *Public Organization Review*, 20(1), 163–177.

Alvehus, J., Eklund, S., and Kastberg, G. (2021). To strengthen or to shatter? On the effects of stratification on professions as systems. *Public Administration*, 99(2), 371–386.

Alvesson, M. (2001). Knowledge work: Ambiguity, image and identity. *Human Relations*, 54(7), 863–886.

Alvesson, M. (2004). *Knowledge Work and Knowledge-Intensive Firms*. Oxford: Oxford University Press.

Alvesson, M. (2013). *The Triumph of Emptiness: Consumption, Higher Education, and Work Organization*. Oxford: Oxford University Press.

Alvesson, M. and Einola, K. (2019). Warning for excessive positivity: Authentic leadership and other traps in leadership studies. *The Leadership Quarterly*, 30, 383–395.

Alvesson, M. and Kärreman, D. (2004). Interfaces of control: Technocratic and socio-ideological control in a global management consultancy firm. *Accounting, Organizations and Society*, 29(3–4), 423–444.

Alvesson, M. and Robertson, M. (2006). The best and the brightest: The construction, significance and effects of elite identities in consulting firms. *Organization*, 13(2), 195–224.

Alvesson, M. and Spicer, A. (2016). *The Stupidity Paradox: The Power and Pitfalls of Functional Stupidity at Work*. London: Profile Books.

Alvesson, M. and Spicer, A. (2019). Neo-institutional theory and organization studies: A mid-life crisis? *Organization Studies*, 40(2), 199–218.

Alvesson, M. and Sveningsson, S. (2008). *Changing Organizational Culture: Cultural Change Work in Progress*. London: Routledge.

Alvesson, M., Gabriel, Y., and Paulsen, R. (2017). *Return to Meaning: A Social Science with Something to Say*. Oxford: Oxford University Press.

Alvesson, M., Kärreman, D., and Sullivan, K. (2015). Professional service firms and identity. In L. Empson, D. Muzio, J.P. Broschak, and B. Hinings (eds), *The Oxford Handbook of Professional Service Firms* (pp 403–424). Oxford: Oxford University Press.

Ammeter, A.P., Douglas, C., Gardner, W.L., Hochwarter, W.A., and Ferris, G.R. (2002). Toward a political theory of leadership. *The Leadership Quarterly*, 13(6), 751–796.

Anderson-Gough, F., Grey, C., and Robson, K. (2000). In the name of the client: The service ethic in two professional services firms. *Human Relations*, 53(9), 1151–1174.

Andersson, T. (2005). *Managers' Identity Work: Experiences from Introspective Management Training*. Göteborg: BAS.

Andersson, T. (2015). The medical leadership challenge in healtchare is an identity challenge. *Leadership in Health Services*, 28(2), 83–99.

Andersson, T. and Gadolin, C. (2020). Understanding institutional work through social interaction in highly institutionalized settings: Lessons from public healthcare organizations. *Scandinavian Journal of Management Online*, 36, 1–10.

Andersson, T. and Liff, R. (2018). Co-optation as a response to competing institutional logics: Professionals and managers in healthcare. *Journal of Professions and Organization*, 5(2), 71–87.

Armour, J. and Sako, M. (2020). AI-enabled business models in legal services: From traditional law firms to next-generation law companies? *Journal of Professions and Organization*, 7(1), 27–46.

Baden-Fuller, C. and Bateson, J. (1990). Promotion strategies for hierarchically organised professional service firms: Is 'up or out' always the best? *International Journal of Service Industry Management*, 1(3), 62–78.

Barley, S.R. (1986). Technology as an occasion for structuring: Evidence from observations of CT scanners and the social order of radiology departments. *Administrative Science Quarterly*, 31(1), 78–108.

REFERENCES

Barley, S.R. (2008). Coalface institutionalism. In R. Greenwood, C. Oliver, K. Sahlin, and R. Suddaby (eds), *The SAGE Handbook of Organizational Institutionalism* (pp 491–518). Los Angeles: SAGE.

Barley, S.R. and Kunda, G. (2001). Bringing work back in. *Organization Science*, 12(1), 76–95.

Barley, S.R. and Kunda, G. (2004). *Gurus, Hired Guns, and Warm Bodies: Itinerant Experts in a Knowledge Economy*. Princeton: Princeton University Press.

Barley, S.R. and Tolbert, P.S. (1997). Institutionalization and structuration: Studying the links between action and institution. *Organization Studies*, 18(1), 93–117.

Battilana, J. and Dorado, S. (2010). Building sustainable hybrid organizations: The case of commercial microfinance organizations. *Academy of Management Journal*, 53(6), 1419–1440.

Bejerot, E. and Hasselbladh, H. (2011). Professional autonomy and pastoral power: The transformation of quality registers in Swedish health care. *Public Administration*, 89(4), 1604–1621.

Bévort, F. and Suddaby, R. (2016). Scripting professional identities: How individuals make sense of contradictory institutional logics. *Journal of Professions and Organization*, 3(1), 17–38.

Bligh, M.C. and Schyns, B. (2007). The romance lives on: Contemporary issues surrounding the romance of leadership. *Leadership*, 3(3), 343–360.

Blomgren, M. and Waks, C. (2015). Coping with contradictions: Hybrid professionals managing institutional complexity. *Journal of Professions and Organization*, 2(1), 78–102.

Blumer, H. (1954). What is wrong with social theory? *American Sociological Review*, 19(1), 3–10.

Bourdieu, P. (1977). *Outline of a Theory of Practice*. Cambridge: Cambridge University Press.

Bourgeault, I.L., Hirschkorn, K., and Sainsaulieu, I. (2011). Relations between professions and organizations: More fully considering the role of the client. *Professions and Professionalism*, 1(1), 67–86.

Boussebaa, M. and Faulconbridge, J.R. (2019). Professional service firms as agents of economic globalization: A political perspective. *Journal of Professions and Organization*, 6, 72–90.

Boussebaa, M., Morgan, G., and Sturdy, A. (2012). Constructing global firms? National, transnational and neocolonial effects in international management consultancies. *Organization Studies*, 33(4), 465–486.

Bowman, J.S. (2000). Towards a professional ethos: From regulatory to reflective codes. *International Review of Administrative Sciences*, 66, 673–687.

Broschak, J.P. (2015). Client relationships in professional service firms. In L. Empson, D. Muzio, J.P. Broschak, and B. Hinings (eds), *The Oxford Handbook of Professional Service Firms* (pp 304–326). Oxford: Oxford University Press.

Brown, J.S. and Duguid, P. (2001). Knowledge and organization: A social-practice perspective. *Organization Science*, 12(2), 198–213.

Brunsson, N. (1989). *The Organization of Hypocrisy: Talk, Decisions, and Actions in Organizations.* Chichester: Wiley.

Brynjolfsson, E. and McAfee, A. (2014). *The Second Machine Age: Work, Progress, and Prosperity in a Time of Brilliant Technologies.* New York: W.W. Norton & Company.

Burawoy, M. (1979). *Manufacturing Consent: Changes in the Labor Process Under Monopoly Capitalism.* Chicago: University of Chicago Press.

Castells, M. (1996). *The Information Age: Economy, Society and Culture. Vol 1. The Rise of the Network Society.* Malden: Blackwell.

Castells, M. (1997). *The Information Age: Economy, Society and Culture. Vol 2. The Power of Identity.* Malden: Blackwell.

Castells, M. (1998). *The Information Age: Economy, Society and Culture. Vol 3. End of Millennium.* Malden: Blackwell.

Catchpole, K.R., De Leval, M.R., McEwan, A., Pigott, N., Elliott, M.J., McQuillan, A. et al (2007). Patient handover from surgery to intensive care: Using Formula 1 pit-stop and aviation models to improve safety and quality. *Pediatric Anesthesia*, 17, 470–478.

Clark, T. (1995). *Managing Consultants: Consultancy as Management of Impressions.* Buckingham: Open University Press.

Coch, L. and French, J.R.P. (1948). Overcoming resistance to change. *Human Relations*, 1(4), 512–532.

Collinson, D., Jones, O.S., and Grint, K. (2018). 'No more heroes': Critical perspectives on leadership romanticism. *Organization Studies*, 39(11), 1625–1647.

Cooper, D.J., Hinings, B., Greenwood, R., and Brown, J.L. (1996). Sedimentation and transformation in organizational change: The case of Canadian law firms. *Organization Studies*, 17(4), 623–647.

Covaleski, M.A., Dirsmith, M.W., Heian, J.B., and Samuel, S. (1998). The calculated and the avowed: Techniques of discipline and struggles over identity in Big Six public accounting firms. *Administrative Science Quarterly*, 43(2), 293–327.

Crevani, L. (2018). Is there leadership in a fluid world? Exploring the ongoing production of direction in organizing. *Leadership*, 14(1), 83–109.

Currie, G. and Spyridonidis, D. (2015). Interpretation of multiple institutional logics on the ground: Actors position, their agency and situational constraints in professionalized contexts. *Organization Studies*, 37(1), 77–97.

Curtis, F. (2001). Ivy-covered exploitation. In J.K. Gibson-Graham, S. Resnick, and R. Wolff (eds), *Re/presenting Class* (pp 81–104). Durham, NC: Duke University Press.

Cushen, J. (2013). Financialization in the workplace: Hegemonic narratives, performative interventions and the angry knowledge worker. *Accounting, Organizations and Society*, 38(4), 314–331.

Czarniawska, B. and Joerges, B. (1995). Winds of organizational change: How ideas translate into objects and actions. *Research in the Sociology of Organizations*, 13, 171–209.

Dan, S. and Pollitt, C. (2015). NPM can work: An optimistic review of the impact of New Public Management reforms in central and eastern Europe. *Public Management Review*, 17(9), 1305–1332.

Deetz, S. (1998). Discursive formations, strategized subordination and self-surveillance. In A. McKinlay and K. Starkey (eds), *Foucault, Management and Organization Theory* (pp 151–172). London: SAGE.

Deetz, S. (2008). Resistance: Would struggle by any other name be as sweet? *Management Communication Quarterly*, 21(3), 387–392.

Denis, J.-L., Langley, A., and Sergi, V. (2012). Leadership in the plural. *The Academy of Management Annals*, 6(1), 211–283.

DeRue, D.S. and Ashford, S.J. (2010). Who will lead and who will follow? A social process of leadership identity construction in organizations. *Academy of Management Review*, 35(4), 627–647.

DiMaggio, P.J. (1988). Interest and agency in institutional theory. In L.G. Zucker (ed), *Institutional Patterns and Organizations: Culture and Environment* (pp 3–22). Cambridge, MA: Ballinger.

DiMaggio, P.J. and Powell, W.J. (1983). The iron cage revisited: Institutional isomorphism and collective rationality in organizational fields. *American Sociological Review*, 48(2), 147–160.

Dirsmith, M.W., Heian, J.B., and Covaleski, M.A. (1997). Structure and agency in an institutionalized setting: The application and social transformation of control in the Big Six. *Accounting, Organizations and Society*, 22(1), 1–27.

Drucker, P.F. (1959). *Landmarks of Tomorrow*. New York: Harper.

Drucker, P.F. (1969). *The Age of Discontinuity: Guidelines to Our Changing Society*. London: Heinemann.

Empson, L. (2017). *Leading Professionals: Power, Politics, and Prima Donnas*. Oxford: Oxford University Press.

Empson, L. and Alvehus, J. (2020). Collective leadership dynamics among professional peers: Co-constructing an unstable equilibrium. *Organization Studies*, 41(9), 1234–1256.

Empson, L. and Chapman, C. (2006). Partnership versus corporation: Implications of alternative forms of governance in professional service firms. *Research in the Sociology of Organizations*, 24, 139–170.

Empson, L., Muzio, D., Broschak, J.B., and Hinings, B. (2015a). Researching professional service firms: An introduction and overview. In L. Empson, D. Muzio, J.B. Broschak, and B. Hinings (eds), *The Oxford Handbook of Professional Service Firms* (pp 1–22). Oxford: Oxford University Press.

Empson, L., Muzio, D., Broschak, J.B., and Hinings, B. (eds) (2015b). *The Oxford Handbook of Professional Service Firms*. Oxford: Oxford University Press.

Evetts, J. (2003). The sociological analysis of professionalism: Occupational change in the modern world. *International Sociology*, 18(2), 395–415.

Evetts, J. (2006). Short note: The sociology of professional groups: New directions. *Current Sociology*, 54(1), 133–143.

Evetts, J. (2011). A new professionalism? Challenges and opportunities. *Current Sociology*, 59(4), 406–422.

Follett, M.P. (2013). *Dynamic Administration: The Collected Papers of Mary Parker Follett*, edited by H.C. Metcalf and L. Urwick. Mansfield Centre: Martino.

Foucault, M. (2008). *The Birth of Biopolitics: Lectures at the Collège de France 1978–1979*. New York: Picador.

Fourcade, M. (2006). The construction of a global profession: The transnationalization of economics. *American Journal of Sociology*, 112(1), 145–194.

Freidson, E. (1985). The reorganization of the medical profession. *Medical Care Review*, 42(1), 11–35.

Freidson, E. (2001). *Professionalism: The Third Logic*. Chicago: University of Chicago Press.

Frey, C.B. and Osborne, M.A. (2013). *The Future of Employment: How Susceptible are Jobs to Computerization?* Oxford Martin School. University of Oxford. Retrieved from: www.oxfordmartin.ox.ac.uk/downloads/academic/The_Future_of_Employment.pdf (accessed 6 July 2021).

Friedland, R. and Alford, R.R. (1991). Bringing society back in: Symbols, practices, and institutional contradictions. In W.W. Powell and P.J. DiMaggio (eds), *The New Institutionalism in Organizational Analysis* (pp 232–263). Chicago: University of Chicago Press.

Gadolin, C., Andersson, T., Eriksson, E., and Hellström, A. (2020). Providing healthcare through 'value shops': Impact on professional fulfilment for physicians and nurses. *International Journal of Health Governance*, 25(2), 127–136.

Garfinkel, H. (1967). *Studies in Ethnomethodology*. Cambridge: Polity.

Geertz, C. (1973). *The Interpretation of Cultures*. New York: Basic Books.

Gibson-Graham, J.K. (1996). *The End of Capitalism (As We Knew It)*. Minneapolis: University of Minnesota Press.

Giddens, A. (1984). *The Constitution of Society: Outline of the Theory of Structuration*. Cambridge: Polity Press.

Goodall, A.H. (2009). *Socrates in the Boardroom: Why Research Universities Should Be Led by Top Scholars*. Princeton: Princeton University Press.

Graeber, D. (2018). *Bullshit Jobs: A Theory*. New York: Simon and Schuster.

Greenwood, R., Hinings, C.R., and Brown, J. (1990). 'P2-form' strategic management: Corporate practices in professional partnerships. *The Academy of Management Journal*, 33(4), 725–755.

Greenwood, R., Raynard, M., Kodeih, F., Micelotta, E.R., and Lounsbury, M. (2011). Institutional complexity and organizational responses. *The Academy of Management Annals*, 5(1), 317–371.

Grey, C. (1994). Career as a project of the self and labour process discipline. *Sociology*, 28(2), 479–497.

Grey, C. (1998). On being a professional in a 'Big Six' firm. *Accounting, Organizations and Society*, 23(5/6), 569–587.

Grint, K. (2010). *Leadership: A Very Short Introduction*. Oxford: Oxford University Press.

Gümüsay, A.A., Claus, L., and Amis, J. (2020). Engaging with grand challenges: An institutional logics perspective. *Organization Theory (Online)*, 1–20.

Gustafsson, A. and Röstlund, L. (2019). *Konsulterna: kampen om Karolinska*. Stockholm: Mondial.

Hägglund, M. (2019). *This Life: Secular Faith and Spiritual Freedom*. New York: Anchor Books.

Haight, A.D. (2001). Burnout, chronic fatigue, and prozac in the professions: The iron law of salaries. *Review of Radical Political Economics*, 33(2), 189–202.

Hallett, T. (2010). The myth incarnate: Recoupling processes, turmoil, and inhabited institutions in an urban elementary school. *American Sociological Review*, 75(1), 52–74.

Hallett, T. and Ventresca, M.J. (2006). Inhabited institutions: Social interactions and organizational forms in Gouldner's *Patterns of Industrial Bureaucracy*. *Theory and Society*, 35(2), 213–236.

Hallonsten, O. (2021). On the essential role of organized skepticism in science's 'internal and lawful autonomy' (Eigengesetzlichkeit). *Journal of Classical Sociology Online*, 1–22.

Hanlon, G. (1996). 'Casino capitalism' and the rise of the 'commercialised' service class: An examination of the accountant. *Critical Perspectives on Accounting*, 7(3), 339–363.

Hanlon, G. (1997). A shifting professionalism: An examination of accountancy. In J. Broadbent, M. Dietrich, and J. Roberts (eds), *The End of the Professions? The Restructuring of Professional Work* (pp 123–139). London: Routledge.

Hood, C. (1991). A public management for all seasons? *Public Administration*, 69(1), 3–19.

Hood, C. (1995). The 'New Public Management' in the 1980s: Variations on a theme. *Accounting, Organizations and Society*, 20(2/3), 93–109.

Jackall, R. (1988). *Moral Mazes: The World of Corporate Managers*. New York: Oxford University Press.

Jarrick, A. and Söderberg, J. (1991). Aktörsstrukturalismen: ett nytt hugg på humanvetenskapens gordiska knut. *Historisk Tidskrift*, 111(1), 59–84.

Karlsson, J.C. (2015). Work, passion, exploitation. *Nordic Journal of Working Life Studies*, 5(2), 3–16.

Kärreman, D., Sveningsson, S., and Alvesson, M. (2002). The return of the machine bureaucracy? Management control in the work settings of professionals. *International Studies of Management and Organization*, 32(2), 70–92.

Kellogg, K.C. (2019). Subordinate activation tactics: Semi-professionals and micro-level institutional change in professional organizations. *Administrative Science Quarterly*, 64(4), 928–975.

Kelly, B. (2013). Policing and security. In P. Erdkamp (ed), *The Cambridge Companion to Ancient Rome* (pp 410–424). Cambridge: Cambridge University Press.

Kirkpatrick, I. (2016). Hybrid managers and professional leadership. In M. Dent, I.L. Bourgeault, J.-L. Denis, and E. Kuhlmann (eds), *The Routledge Companion to the Professions and Professionalism* (pp 175–187). New York: Routledge.

Kirkpatrick, I. and Noordegraaf, M. (2015). Organizations and occupations: Towards hybrid professionalism in professional service firms? In L. Empson, D. Muzio, J.P. Broschack, and B. Hinings (eds), *The Oxford Handbook of Professional Service Firms* (pp 92–112). Oxford: Oxford University Press.

Kirkpatrick, I., Sturdy, A., Alvarado, N.R., Blanco-Oliver, A., and Veronesi, G. (2019). The impact of management consultants on public service efficiency. *Policy and Politics*, 47(1), 77–95.

Klintman, M. (2019). *Knowledge Resistance: How We Avoid Insight From Others*. Manchester: Manchester University Press.

Kodeih, F. and Greenwood, R. (2014). Responding to institutional complexity: The role of identity. *Organization Studies*, 35(1), 7–39.

Kor, Y.Y. and Leblebici, H. (2005). How do interdependencies among human-capital deployment, development, and diversification strategies affect firms' financial performance? *Strategic Management Journal*, 26(10), 967–985.

Kornberger, M., Justesen, L. and Mouritsen, J. (2011). 'When you make manager, we put a big mountain in front of you': An ethnography of managers in a Big 4 accounting firm. *Accounting, Organizations and Society*, 36(8), 514–533.

Kosík, K. (1976). *Dialectics of the Concrete: A Study on Problems of Man and World*. Dordrecht: Reidel.

Krause, E.A. (1996). *Death of the Guilds: Professions, States, and the Advance of Capitalism, 1930 to the Present*. New Haven: Yale University Press.

Kronblad, C. (2020). How digitalization changes our understanding of professional service firms. *Academy of Management Discoveries*, 6(3), 436–454.

Larson, M.S. (1977). *The Rise of Professionalism: A Sociological Analysis*. Berkeley: University of California Press.

Latour, B. (1986). The powers of association. In J. Law (ed), *Power, Action and Belief: A New Sociology of Knowledge?* (pp 264–280). London: Routledge and Kegan Paul.

Latour, B. (1991). Technology is society made durable. In J. Law (ed), *A Sociology of Monsters: Essays on Power, Technology and Domination* (pp 103–131). *Sociological Review*, special issue.

Lave, J. and Wenger, E. (1991). *Situated Learning: Legitimate Peripheral Participation*. Cambridge: Cambridge University Press.

Lawrence, T.B. and Suddaby, R. (2006). Institutions and institutional work. In S.R. Clegg, C. Hardy, T.B. Lawrence, and W.B. Nord (eds), *The SAGE Handbook of Organization Studies* (2nd edn, pp 215–254). London: SAGE.

Legge, K. (2005). *Human Resource Management: Rhetorics and Realities* (anniversary edn). London: Palgrave Macmillan.

Lester, S. (2020). New technology and professional work. *Professions and Professionalism*, 10(1), 1–15.

Levay, C. and Waks, C. (2009). Professions and the pursuit of transparency in healthcare: Two cases of soft autonomy. *Organization Studies*, 30(5), 509–527.

Liu, J. (2013). Professional associations. In P. Erdkamp (ed), *The Cambridge Companion to Ancient Rome* (pp 352–368). Cambridge: Cambridge University Press.

Llewellyn, S. (2001). 'Two-way windows': Clinicians as medical managers. *Organization Studies*, 22(4), 593–623.

Løwendahl, B.R. (2005). *Strategic Management of Professional Service Firms* (3rd edn). Copenhagen: Copenhagen Business School Press.

Lupu, I. and Empson, L. (2015). Illusio and overwork: Playing the game in the accounting field. *Accounting, Auditing and Accountability Journal*, 28(8), 1310–1340.

Maister, D.H. (1993). *Managing the Professional Service Firm*. New York: The Free Press.

Maister, D.H. (2004). The anatomy of a consulting firm. In C.J. Fombrun and M.D. Nevins (eds), *The Advice Business: Essential Tools and Models for Management Consulting*. Upper Saddle River: Pearson.

March, J.G. (1994). *A Primer on Decision Making: How Decisions Happen*. New York: The Free Press.

March, J.G. and Olsen, J.P. (2011). The logic of appropriateness. In R.E. Goodin (ed), *The Oxford Handbook of Political Science* (pp 478–497). Oxford: Oxford University Press.

McIntyre, L. (2018). *Post-Truth*. Cambridge, MA: The MIT Press.

McPherson, C.M. and Sauder, M. (2013). Logics in action: Managing institutional complexity in a drug court. *Administrative Science Quarterly*, 58(2), 165–196.

Meindl, J.R., Ehrlich, S.B., and Dukerich, J.M. (1985). The romance of leadership. *Administrative Science Quarterly*, 30(1), 78–102.

Merton, R.K. (1968). *Social Theory and Social Structure*. New York: The Free Press.

Meyer, J.W. and Rowan, B. (1977). Institutionalized organizations: Formal structure as myth and ceremony. *American Journal of Sociology*, 83(2), 340–363.

Meyer, R.E., Jancsary, D., and Höllerer, M.A. (2021). Zones of meaning, *Leitideen*, institutional logics – and practices: A phenomenological institutional perspective on shared meaning structures. *Research in the Sociology of Organizations*, 70, 161–186.

Michel, A. (2011). Transcending socialization: A nine-year ethnography of the body's role in organizational control and knowledge workers' transformation. *Administrative Science Quarterly*, 56(3), 325–368.

Mills, C.W. (1951/2002). *White Collar: The American Middle Classes*. Oxford: Oxford University Press.

Mills, C.W. (1959/2000). *The Sociological Imagination*. Oxford: Oxford University Press.

Mintzberg, H. (1979). *The Structuring of Organizations: A Synthesis of the Research*. Englewood Cliffs: Prentice Hall.

Mintzberg, H. (1983). *Structure in Fives: Designing Effective Organizations*. Upper Saddle River: Prentice Hall.

Morris, T. and Empson, L. (1998). Organisation and expertise: An exploration of knowledge bases and the management of accounting and consulting firms. *Accounting, Organizations and Society*, 23(5/6), 609–624.

Muzio, D., Aulakh, S., and Kirkpatrick, I. (2019). *Professional Occupations and Organizations*. Cambridge: Cambridge University Press.

Muzio, D., Faulconbridge, J., Gabbioneta, C., and Greenwood, R. (2016). Bad apples, bad barrels and bad cellars: A 'boundaries' perspective on professional misconduct. In D. Palmer, K. Smith-Crowe, and R. Greenwood (eds), *Organizational Wrongdoing: Key Perspectives and New Directions* (pp 141–175). Cambridge: Cambridge University Press.

Noordegraaf, M. (2020). Protective or connective professionalism? How connected professionals can (still) act as autonomous and authoritative experts. *Journal of Professions and Organization*, 7(2), 205–223.

Ocasio, W., Thornton, P.H., and Lounsbury, M. (2017). Advances to the institutional logics perspective. In R. Greenwood, C. Oliver, T.B. Lawrence, and R.E. Meyer (eds), *The SAGE Handbook of Organizational Institutionalism* (2nd edn, pp 509–531). London: SAGE.

Oppenheimer, M. (1972). The proletarianization of the professional. *The Sociology Review Monograph*, 20(1_suppl), 213–227.

Ouchi, W.G. (1979). A conceptual framework for the design of organizational control mechanisms. *Management Science*, 25(9), 833–848.

Pache, A.C. and Santos, F. (2013). Inside the hybrid organization: Selective coupling as a response to competing institutional logics. *Academy of Management Journal*, 56(4), 972–1001.

Pfeffer, J. (1981). *Power in Organizations*. Cambridge, MA: Ballinger.

Piketty, T. (2014). *Capital in the Twenty-First Century*. Cambridge, MA: Belknap Press.

Polanyi, M. (1966). *The Tacit Dimension*. Gloucester: Peter Smith.

Pomerantsev, P. (2014). *Nothing Is True and Everything Is Possible: The Surreal Heart of the New Russia*. New York: Public Affairs.

Power, M. (1997). *The Audit Society: Rituals of Verification*. Oxford: Oxford University Press.

Proctor, R.N. (2008). Agnothology: A missing term to describe the cultural production of ignorance (and its study). In R.N. Proctor and L. Schiebinger (eds), *Agnothology: The Making and Unmaking of Ignorance* (pp 1–34). Stanford: Stanford University Press.

Reay, T. and Hinings, C.R.B. (2009). Managing the rivalry of competing institutional logics. *Organization Studies*, 30(6), 629–652.

Reay, T. and Jones, C. (2016). Qualitatively capturing institutional logics. *Strategic Organization*, 14(4), 441–454.

Rolandsson, B., Alasoini, T., Berglund, T., Dølvik, J.E., Hedenus, A., Ilsøe, A. et al (2020). *Digital Transformations of Traditional Work in the Nordic Countries*. Copenhagen: Nordic Council of Ministers.

Rose, N. (1999). *Governing the Soul: The Shaping of the Private Self*. London: Free Association Books.

Rost, J.C. (1993). *Leadership for the Twenty-First Century*. Westport: Praeger.

Sahlin, K. and Eriksson-Zetterquist, U. (2016). Collegiality in modern universities: The composition of governance ideals and practices. *Nordic Journal of Studies in Educational Policy*, 2–3, 33640.

Sandberg, J. (2000). Understanding human competence at work: An interpretive approach. *Academy of Management Journal*, 43(1), 9–25.

Santos, S. (2018). Becoming a lawyer in a large law firm: The idea of the unstoppable worker. *Professions and Professionalism*, 8(3), 1–15.

Schedlitzki, D. and Edwards, G. (2018). *Studying Leadership: Traditional and Critical Approaches* (2nd edn). London: SAGE.

Schön, D.A. (1983). *The Reflective Practitioner: How Professionals Think in Action*. New York: Basic Books.

Scott, R.W. (1965). Reactions to supervision in a heteronomous professional organization. *Administrative Science Quarterly*, 10(1), 65–81.

Sennett, R. (2008). *The Craftsman*. London: Penguin.

Sharma, A. (1997). Professional as agent: Knowledge asymmetry in agency exchange. *Academy of Management Review*, 22(3), 758–798.

Sherer, P.D. (1995). Leveraging human assets in law firms: Human capital structures and organizational capabilities. *ILR Review*, 48(4), 671–691.

Skålén, P. (2018). *Service Logic*. Lund: Studentlitteratur.

Smets, M. and Jarzabkowski, P. (2013). Reconstructing institutional complexity in practice: A relational model of institutional work and complexity. *Human Relations*, 66(10), 1279–1309.

Smets, M., Jarzabkowski, P., Burke, G.T., and Spee, P. (2015). Reinsurance trading in Lloyd's of London: Balancing conflicting-yet-complementary logics in practice. *Academy of Management Journal*, 58(3), 932–970.

Snook, S.A. (2000). *Friendly Fire: The Accidental Shootdown of U.S. Black Hawks Over Northern Iraq*. Princeton: Princeton University Press.

Stabell, C.B. and Fjeldstad, Ø.D. (1998). Configuring value for competitive advantage: On chains, shops, and networks. *Strategic Management Journal*, 19, 413–437.

Standing, G. (2011). *The Precariat: The New Dangerous Class*. New York: Bloomsbury Academic.

Sturdy, A. (1997). The consultancy process: An insecure business? *Journal of Management Studies*, 34(3), 389–413.

Sturdy, A. and Wright, C. (2011). The active client: The boundary-spanning roles of internal consultants as gatekeepers, brokers and partners of their external counterparts. *Management Learning*, 42(5), 485–503.

Styhre, A. (2013). *Professionals Making Judgments*. Basingstoke: Palgrave Macmillan.

Susskind, R. and Susskind, D. (2015). *The Future of the Professions: How Technology Will Transform the Work of Human Experts*. Oxford: Oxford University Press.

Svensson, L.G. and Östnäs, A. (1990). *Rummens psykologer – själarnas arkitekter: en studie av professionella i arbete*. Stockholm: Carlsson.

Tegmark, M. (2017). *Life 3.0: Being Human in the Age of Artificial Intelligence*. New York: Alfred A. Knopf.

Terkel, S. (1974). *Working: People Talk About What They Do All Day and How They Feel About What They Do*. New York: Pantheon.

Thornton, P.H. (2004). *Markets from Culture: Institutional Logics and Organizational Decisions in Higher Education Publishing*. Stanford: Stanford University Press.

Thornton, P.H. and Ocasio, W. (2008). Institutional logics. In R. Greenwood, C. Oliver, K. Sahlin, and R. Suddaby (eds), *The SAGE Handbook of Organizational Institutionalism* (pp 99–129). Los Angeles: SAGE.

Thornton, P.H., Ocasio, W., and Lounsbury, M. (2012). *The Institutional Logics Perspective: A New Approach to Culture, Structure, and Process.* Oxford: Oxford University Press.

Tolkien, J.R.R. (1954/1994). *The Fellowship of the Ring.* New York: Random House.

Tourish, D. (2019). *Management Studies in Crisis: Fraud, Deception and Meaningless Research.* Cambridge: Cambridge University Press.

Townley, B. (1993). Foucault, power/knowledge, and its relevance for human resource management. *Academy of Management Review*, 18(3), 518–545.

Verbeeten, F.H.M. and Speklé, R.F. (2015). Management control, results-oriented culture and public sector performance: Empirical evidence on New Public Management. *Organization Studies*, 36(7), 953–978.

von Nordenflycht, A. (2010). What is a professional service firm? Toward a theory and taxonomy of knowledge-intensive firms. *Academy of Management Review*, 35(1), 155–174.

Waisbord, S. (2013). *Reinventing Professionalism: Journalism and News in Global Perspective.* Cambridge: Polity.

Wallace, J.E. (1995). Organizational and professional commitment in professional and nonprofessional organizations. *Administrative Science Quarterly*, 40(2), 228–255.

Waring, J. (2014). Restratification, hybridity and professional elites: Questions of power, identity and relational contingency at the points of 'professional–organisational intersection'. *Sociology Compass*, 8(5), 688–704.

Waring, J. and Bishop, S. (2013). McDonaldization or commercial re-stratification: Corporatization and the multimodal organisation of English doctors. *Social Science and Medicine*, 82, 147–155.

Watson, T.J. (2001). *In Search of Management: Culture, Chaos and Control in Managerial Work.* Andover: Cengage.

Watson, T.J. (2002). Professions and professionalism: Should we jump off the bandwagon, better to study where it is going? *International Studies of Management and Organization*, 32(2), 93–105.

Weatherford, J. (2004). *Genghis Khan and the Making of the Modern World.* New York: Broadway Books.

Weber, M. (1915/1946). Religious rejections of the world and their directions. In H.H. Gerth and C.W. Mills (eds), *From Max Weber: Essays in Sociology* (pp 323–359). New York: Oxford University Press.

Weber, M. (1968). *Economy and Society. Vol. 1.* Berkeley: University of California Press.

Weick, K.E. (1976). Educational organizations as loosely coupled systems. *Administrative Science Quarterly*, 21(1), 1–19.

Werr, A., Stjernberg, T., and Docherty, P. (1997). The functions of methods of change in management consulting. *Journal of Organizational Change Management*, 10(4), 288–307.

Wilensky, H.L. (1964). The professionalization of everyone? *The American Journal of Sociology*, 70(2), 137–158.

Winroth, K. (1999). *När management kom till advokatbyrån*. Göteborg: BAS.

Woodward, J. (1965). *Industrial Organization: Theory and Practice*. London: Oxford University Press.

Zaleznik, A. (1977). Managers and leaders: Are they different? *Harvard Business Review* 82(4), 74–81.

Zilber, T.B. (2013). Institutional logics and institutional work: Should they be agreed? *Research in the Sociology of Organizations*, 39A, 77–96.

Zuboff, S. (1988). *In the Age of the Smart Machine: The Future of Work and Power*. New York: Basic Books.

Zuboff, S. (2019). *The Age of Surveillance Capitalism: The Fight for a Human Future at the New Frontier of Power*. London: Profile Books.

Index